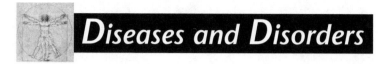
Diseases and Disorders

Mad Cow Disease

Diseases and Disorders

Mad Cow Disease

Titles in the Diseases and Disorders series include:

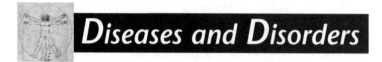

Diseases and Disorders

Mad Cow Disease

by Barbara Sheen

LUCENT BOOKS

An imprint of Thomson Gale, a part of The Thomson Corporation

THOMSON
━━━✳━━━ ™
GALE

Detroit • New York • San Francisco • San Diego • New Haven, Conn.
Waterville, Maine • London • Munich

On Cover: An electron micrograph reveals abnormal proteins called prions
speckling a cell's surface; prions cause mad cow disease.

© 2005 Thomson Gale, a part of The Thomson Corporation.

Thomson and Star Logo are trademarks and Gale and Lucent Books are registered trademarks used
herein under license.

For more information, contact
Lucent Books
27500 Drake Rd.
Farmington Hills, MI 48331-3535
Or you can visit our Internet site at http://www.gale.com

LIBRARY OF CONGRESS CATALOGING-IN-PUBLICATION DATA

Sheen, Barbara.
    Mad cow disease / by Barbara Sheen.
        p. cm. — (Diseases and disorders)
Includes bibliographical references and index.
Contents: A mysterious disease—From cows to humans—A killer protein—Protecting
the public—What the future holds.
    ISBN 1-59018-635-4 (hard cover : alk. paper)
    1. Prion diseases—Juvenile literature. 2. Bovine spongiform encephalopathy—
Juvenile literature. I. Title. II. Series: Diseases and disorders series.
    RA644.P93S53 2004
    616.8'3—dc22
                                                            2004010684

Printed in the United States of America

Table of Contents

"The Most Difficult Puzzles Ever Devised"

CHARLES BEST, ONE of the pioneers in the search for a cure for diabetes, once explained what it is about medical research that intrigued him so. "It's not just the gratification of knowing one is helping people," he confided, "although that probably is a more heroic and selfless motivation. Those feelings may enter in, but truly, what I find best is the feeling of going toe to toe with nature, of trying to solve the most difficult puzzles ever devised. The answers are there somewhere, those keys that will solve the puzzle and make the patient well. But how will those keys be found?"

Since the dawn of civilization, nothing has so puzzled people—and often frightened them, as well—as the onset of illness in a body or mind that had seemed healthy before. A seizure, the inability of a heart to pump, the sudden deterioration of muscle tone in a small child—being unable to reverse such conditions or even to understand why they occur was unspeakably frustrating to healers. Even before there were names for such conditions, even before they were understood at all, each was a reminder of how complex the human body was, and how vulnerable.

While our grappling with understanding diseases has been frustrating at times, it has also provided some of humankind's most heroic accomplishments. Alexander Fleming's accidental discovery in 1928 of a mold that could be turned into penicillin has resulted in the saving of untold millions of lives. The isolation of the enzyme insulin has reversed what was once a death sentence for anyone with diabetes. There have been great strides in combating conditions for which there is not yet a cure, too. Medicines can help AIDS patients live longer, diagnostic tools such as mammography and ultrasounds can help doctors find tumors while they are treatable, and laser surgery techniques have made the most intricate, minute operations routine.

This "toe-to-toe" competition with diseases and disorders is even more remarkable when seen in a historical continuum. An astonishing amount of progress has been made in a very short time. Just two hundred years ago, the existence of germs as a cause of some diseases was unknown. In fact, it was less than 150 years ago that a British surgeon named Joseph Lister had difficulty persuading his fellow doctors that washing their hands before delivering a baby might increase the chances of a healthy delivery (especially if they had just attended to a diseased patient)!

Each book in Lucent's Diseases and Disorders series explores a disease or disorder and the knowledge that has been accumulated (or discarded) by doctors through the years. Each book also examines the tools used for pinpointing a diagnosis, as well as the various means that are used to treat or cure a disease. Finally, new ideas are presented—techniques or medicines that may be on the horizon.

Frustration and disappointment are still part of medicine, for not every disease or condition can be cured or prevented. But the limitations of knowledge are being pushed outward constantly; the "most difficult puzzles ever devised" are finding challengers every day.

A Rare Disease

MAD COW DISEASE is a fatal illness that affects the brain and central nervous system of cattle. The disease, which caused an epidemic in British cattle in the 1980s and 1990s, can be transmitted to humans who eat infected beef. The human form of mad cow disease is fatal but very rare, especially when it is compared with more common diseases such as cancer or heart disease. Although the idea of becoming fatally ill from eating a hamburger is frightening, the reality is that the human form of mad cow disease is not easy to contract. Indeed, although more than two hundred thousand cows in Great Britain were infected with mad cow disease and millions of people probably ate infected beef, as of March 2004, only 140 people in the world had died of the human form of the disease.

Something to Worry About?

Not all cuts of meat spread mad cow disease. Muscle meat such as that found in steaks and roasts is unlikely to be infected. Similarly, milk from infected dairy cows does not pose any risk. This is because the infectious agent that causes mad cow disease is rarely found in a cow's muscles or in the parts of a cow involved in milk production.

On the other hand, meat that contains nerve tissue and comes from a cow's brain, lymph glands, tonsils, or spinal cord is more likely to be infected. These are the parts of the cow where the infectious agent that causes mad cow disease is found. Ground beef and sausage, which are composed of meat taken from multiple parts of the cow, may on occasion include meat from the brain and spinal cord. In addition, the meat used to make ground beef and sausage is not usually composed of meat from just one cow. Instead, meat from hundreds of cows is combined to form these products. It is possible that meat from one hundred cows may be used in one hamburger. This raises the odds of contaminated beef being used. Therefore, hamburgers, meat loaf, meat pies, and sauage have been implicated in mad cow disease.

However, even these cuts of meat are not likely to be infected if they come from cattle younger than two years old. Young cows have not been shown to develop mad cow disease. This may be another reason why the human form of the disease is rare, as most meat products come from younger cows.

Genetics may also account for why mad cow disease is so rare in humans. Thus far, all humans who contracted mad cow disease were found to have a particular gene that occurs in about 37 percent of the world's Caucasian population. The gene rarely appears in other races. Scientists cannot say for certain whether the presence of this gene makes people more susceptible to contracting the human form of mad cow disease, but they do think there is a connection. Based on this, scientists theorize that people who do not have this gene are better able to fight off human mad cow disease and are thus less likely to develop the disease.

Because the disease is so rare, most Americans knew little about mad cow disease

Ground beef may contain meat from a hundred different cattle, increasing the risk of contamination.

After hearing reports of just one case of mad cow disease in the United States, some Americans stopped buying beef.

until 1996, when the media reported that ten people in Great Britain had contracted the human form of the disease. As the news spread, concerns about food safety followed. So, too, did concerns about whether the government and food industry were doing enough to protect the public. However, because the disease had never been seen in North America, most Americans felt secure.

Then, in 2003, a single case of mad cow disease was discovered in the United States. This one case caused panic. Many people began to boycott beef and beef by-products. Because eating infected meat can be deadly, some people now wonder whether it is safe to eat beef. "I'm standing in my grocery's meat department paralyzed with indecision," one consumer explains. "I should be shopping for dinner, but I can't, because I just don't know what's safe anymore. Seems like just a few months ago, food safety wasn't an issue."[1]

Food safety is indeed a concern when eating contaminated ground beef and sausage, and resulting illness can wreak devastation on individuals and their families. The human form of mad cow disease affects a person's mind and body. It causes healthy, active people to become as helpless as infants. Early psychiatric symptoms quickly deteriorate to the point at which patients can no longer recognize their family or friends, while physically patients become unable to perform the most basic actions. The brains of people with mad cow disease literally waste away, and death is usually unavoidable. The anguish this causes to patients and their families is staggering.

Understanding the Disease

The best way to help lessen people's anxiety and make sure the disease's victims have not died in vain is to learn more about mad cow disease. Learning what causes the disease and how the infection is transmitted to cattle and then to humans will help experts develop a plan to prevent the disease from occurring in animals, as well as point the way to effective treatments. This knowledge will also help consumers make informed decisions about food safety. The father of a human mad cow disease patient explains: "If we had known any different, my daughter would not be in this position today."[2]

Chapter 1

A Mysterious Disease

BOVINE SPONGIFORM ENCEPHALOPATHY (BSE), or mad cow disease, first appeared in cows in Great Britain in the early 1980s. It posed a mystery to physicians and scientists because it was an emerging disease, which means it had never been encountered before.

A Sick Cow

In 1985 an eight-year-old cow raised on Plurenden Manor, a dairy farm in Kent, England, came down with a strange illness. The cow trembled, lost weight, staggered when she walked, and kicked and nipped at the farmer and the other cows. This combination of symptoms had never been seen before. Cows sometimes act aggressively due to ovarian cysts or lack of magnesium, but neither problem causes a cow to tremble or become uncoordinated. Colin Whitaker, the attending veterinarian, describes the cow's symptoms:

> When you approached her, she would shy away. She was previously a quiet cow and had started becoming aggressive, rather nervous, knocking other cows, bashing other cows and so on and becoming rather dangerous to handle. She would also at the same time become rather uncoordinated. If you shooed her, she would stumble, particularly on the back legs, and go down, and then scrabble along.[3]

When Whitaker examined the cow, he could not find any signs of disease. Her temperature was normal, as was her white blood count. There was no redness or swelling anywhere on her body, nor was there an excess of fluids such as mucus or pus. These symptoms are all signs of inflammation, which is the way the body responds to infectious foreign organisms. Healthy animals and humans do not exhibit these symptoms because their bodies are not under attack by infectious agents. However, inflammation or not, the cow was not healthy.

Without any sign of infection, it was impossible to determine what was causing the cow's illness. This made it difficult to prescribe an effective treatment. Whitaker tried a number of different treatments without success. Antibiotics, anti-inflammatory drugs, medication for ovarian cysts, antidotes for poison, and magnesium supplements all proved ineffective. Tom Forsyth, the

Normally placid cows such as these become aggressive, nervous, and uncoordinated when stricken with mad cow disease.

head stockman at Plurenden Manor explains: "We considered a whole range of possible causes, from lead poisoning to rabies, but nothing made sense. We did not know where it was coming from and we did not know how to put it right."[4]

The cow's condition continued to worsen, proving to be fatal. Within the next few months, seven more cows at Plurenden Manor came down with the same fatal illness. Whitaker assumed that whatever was causing the disease was limited to Plurendon Manor. He recalls: "I had no inkling of the potential scale of it. If someone had told me then of the panic that would be caused, or that there would be 150,000 cases of BSE in 10 years' time, I would have thought they were mad."[5]

Transmissible Spongiform Encephalopathy

Indeed, the disease was not limited to Plurenden Manor. Similar cases began cropping up across England and Wales. By the end of 1987, 420 cows had died of the strange disease, and there appeared to be no end in sight. All the affected cows exhibited the same symptoms. All were adults, and all died of the disease or were put down because of it.

It was clear that, in order to stop the spread of the disease, scientists needed to learn more about it. Because the ill cows showed no signs of infection, running tests on live subjects did not provide any clues. Therefore, in 1986 the British Ministry of Agriculture Fisheries and Food began performing autopsies on the vital organs of cows killed by the mysterious disease. The organs were examined under high-power electron microscopes at the Central Veterinary Laboratory in Surrey, England. In every case, the cow's brain was riddled with holes. This gave the brain a spongy appearance similar to a household sponge or a slice of Swiss cheese. The greatest mass of holes was found in the cerebellum, the part of the brain that controls balance and muscle coordination. This explained the affected cows' lack of coordination. There were also spongy holes across a part of the brain known as the cerebral cortex. This part of the brain is believed to control thought, emotion, behavior, and memory. These holes could have been responsible for the cows' aggressive behavior.

Scientists noted that the holes formed a flowerlike pattern surrounded by hard clumps of protein.

The only other times scientists had seen similar spongy holes was in brains affected by a group of puzzling diseases known as transmissible spongiform encephalopathies, or TSEs. These diseases, which affect animals and people, were given this name because they can be transmitted from victim to victim and cause spongy holes to form in the brain. The holes slowly destroy brain cells and neurons, making it impossible for messages to be transmitted to the body. The destruction is gradual, silent, and almost always fatal. Indeed it can take anywhere from a few months to three or four decades for visible symptoms, such as problems with movement and behavior, to appear. But once symptoms appear, the duration of the illness is usually short, with death typically occurring within three months to a year.

Transmissible spongiform encephalopathy (TSE), the scientific term for diseases like mad cow disease, refers to the spongy holes that develop in the sick animal's brain.

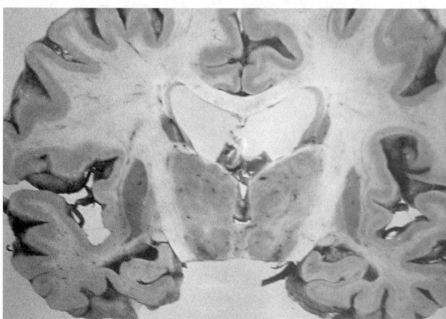

Wild deer and elk, domestic sheep, and mink (pictured) are among the animals that can contract a form of TSE.

TSEs in Animals

There are a number of different TSEs that affect animals. Because they are similar to mad cow disease, understanding them helped scientists untangle what was happening to the cows in Great Britain. One animal TSE, mink spongiform encephalopathy, for example, affects mink. It most often develops on mink farms, where these animals are raised for their fur. Chronic wasting disease, another TSE, affects deer and elk. As its name implies, the disease causes animals to lose so much weight they, quite literally, seem to waste away. The disease is found throughout the United States. A major outbreak occurred in Wisconsin in 2002.

The most common animal TSE is called scrapie, which affects sheep. It has been found in Europe for more than 250 years. It first appeared in the United States in 1947. Currently it affects sheep in every country in the world except Australia and New Zealand.

Sheep with scrapie exhibit symptoms very similar to those of the cows in Great Britain. In addition, scrapie causes sheep to itch so intensely that they scrape their flanks against trees, gates, and fences, often scraping off both their wool and the skin underneath. Philip Yam, the author of *The Pathological Protein*, describes scrapie in this way: "Infected animals may develop intense itchiness and go out of their way to find posts and fences against which to rub. . . . By the time a sheep succumbs—usually in one to six months after the onset of symptoms—most of its fleece may have been scratched off, leaving gaping sores."[6]

Human TSEs

There are also two rare TSEs that affect humans. They too are similar to the cow disease. Therefore scientists examined these human TSEs in an effort to solve the mystery of what was happening to the cows in Great Britain, and later to humans.

One human TSE is a disease called Creutzfeldt-Jakob disease or CJD. CJD usually affects people over sixty-five years old. It is an uncommon disease that appears to develop spontaneously, affecting approximately one in every 1 million people. In addition, a few cases of CJD were acquired when individuals came in contact with medical equipment infected with CJD. But this type of transmission is quite rare.

CJD causes movement problems similar to those displayed by the cows in Great Britain. In addition, as in the cow disease, CJD causes changes in behavior. People with CJD appear to be dazed and depressed and suffer from memory loss. Hans Gerhard Creutzfeldt describes the mental state of Bertha, the first person to be diagnosed with the disease: "She no longer wanted to eat or bathe. . . . Only rarely were sensible answers to be obtained from her. She became emaciated and could not walk or stand without help, and she mostly presented a dazed, stupefied expression."[7]

The other human TSE, kuru, is a disease that affected natives of the South Pacific island of New Guinea during the 1950s and 1960s. Like the cow disease, its symptoms include weight loss, trembling, poor coordination, and muscle spasms that cause patients to shriek or laugh uncontrollably. These symptoms progressively worsen until the victims die. People with kuru lose control of all their voluntary muscles, including their ability to stand, move about, or speak. Eventually they become completely paralyzed and lose their ability to swallow. Death follows. Carleton Gajdusek, Nobel Prize winner for his work on kuru, describes a kuru patient:

> One child, a boy of about seven, had been carried here; he is obviously unlikely to survive for long, can no longer walk, has hardly distinguishable speech, and urinates and defecates in the house. . . . As with all cases, he has to be fed now, having lost the ability to bring food to his mouth. It is hard to believe he is a recent case—a boy previously of normal intelligence and physical development—but multiple reliable informants testify that he was walking, running, and playing normally only three months ago.[8]

Making Connections

Although no one knows what causes TSEs, how they develop, or how they are transmitted, scientists know more about kuru than other TSEs, animal or human. They theorize that kuru developed and was transmitted as a result of cannibalism. Therefore, in an effort to find out why cows in Great Britain were becoming ill, scientists looked more closely at how kuru developed.

At the beginning of the twentieth century the Fore, a native tribe of New Guinea, practiced cannibalism. When someone died, his or her body was butchered; cooked with salt, ginger, and vegetable greens; and then eaten. This practice was considered a way to honor the dead person.

Forms of Transmissible Spongiform Encephalopathy (TSE)

Form of TSE	Affected species	Cause	When infection first detected
Scrapie	Sheep	Infectious agent unknown; may be diet-based	In Britain during the last 250 years; in the United States since 1947; known in most countries worldwide
Bovine spongiform encephalopathy (BSE), or mad cow disease	Cows	Most likely through a food supplement that contained scrapie-infected sheep parts	1986 in British cattle
Transmissible mink encephalopathy (TME)	Mink	Possibly through sheep with scrapie	First U.S. outbreak in 1947
Kuru	Humans	Cannibalistic rituals using deceased relatives	Early 1900s Papua New Guinea in a tribe called Fore
Creutzfeldt-Jakob disease (CJD)	Humans	Naturally occurring in one of every million people worldwide; mostly affects 50- to 75-year-olds	1920
New variant Creutzfeldt-Jakob disease (vCJD) (human BSE)	Humans	Most likely through eating meat products infected with BSE from cows	1994–1995 in young adults who fell ill

Source: www.pbs.org.

By the 1950s a strange disease began affecting the Fore. The Fore named it *kuru*, which means "to tremble" in their language. Scientists investigating the disease were baffled by it. Although, similar to the cow disease, sick patients showed no signs of infection, scientists knew the disease was infectious. Gajdusek proved this.

In the 1950s and 1960s natives of New Guinea suffered from a form of TSE called kuru. Medical researchers believe it was transmitted through cannibalism.

In an attempt to determine whether kuru was infectious, Gajdusek injected kuru-infected brain tissue into the brains of healthy laboratory chimpanzees. When the chimps developed symptoms, including tremors, lack of balance, weight loss, and uncontrollable shrieks, it was clear that kuru was indeed infectious. Postmortem examinations also made it clear that the brains of kuru victims were riddled with spongy holes similar to those of individuals with CJD. What was unclear was how the disease was transmitted. In order to solve this mystery, scientists examined several factors, including the eating habits of the Fore.

Scientists theorized that at one point the Fore ate the brain tissue of a person infected with CJD and contracted the disease. The infectious agent that caused CJD mutated slightly in these people, taking decades to kill them. They, in turn, were eaten and the new mutated form of CJD, which became kuru, was passed on again. As more infected people were eaten, the new disease became more powerful. And, because the Fore women and children ate brain tissue, this group was hardest hit. The men, who usually did not eat brain tissue, were not as affected. Although this theory has never been proven, the disease declined once the Fore stopped practicing cannibalism.

Bovine Spongiform Encephalopathy

In trying to make connections between the cow disease and TSEs and solve the mystery of how the cow disease developed, scientists compared the brains of stricken cows to those of animals with TSEs. And because the symptoms of kuru and scrapie most

The spongelike patterns in the brain of a cow with bovine spongiform encephalopathy (BSE) differ from those in other forms of TSE.

resembled those of the cows, they focused their attention on the link with these diseases.

The scientists found that although all TSEs have similar symptoms and all cause spongy holes in the brain, few form a flowerlike pattern surrounded by protein deposits. Only two do—kuru and scrapie. But neither of these diseases is exactly the same as the cow disease. There are small differences. First, the symptoms are somewhat different. Infected cows do not make strange noises as kuru patients do. Nor do they scratch themselves repeatedly as do sheep with scrapie. Second, under close examination the damage to the brain is also somewhat different. For example, the flowerlike pattern in the cows' brains is rounded, while the pattern is more angular in the brains of animals with scrapie and kuru. In addition, fewer spongy holes and more large plaque deposits characterize the cows' brains, while the reverse is true in scrapie.

Scientists decided that what they were seeing was a new TSE. They named the new disease bovine spongiform encephalopathy, or BSE. The media dubbed it "mad cow disease" because of the way it affected a cow's behavior. Pathologist Gerald Wells, who examined some of the cows' brains, recalls: "Each of the . . . cases I examined had a common novel pathology [a characteristic], with the essential change being a . . . spongy transformation of the brain. . . . Compared with most other animal disorders the changes most resembled scrapie, but there were subtle differences."[9]

Crossing the Species Barrier

Classifying the new disease as BSE, however, did not help experts determine why the cows developed the disease or how to prevent the disease from spreading. Because kuru is transmitted when victims eat diseased tissue, scientists looked at what cows were eating. It was commonly accepted that kuru developed from the consumption of tissue infected with CJD, a human disease. As there had never been a TSE in cows from which BSE might have developed, scientists were baffled about what the cows could have eaten to lead to the development of mad cow disease. They

Nobel laureate Carleton Gajdusek discovered that infectious diseases like TSE can be transmitted across species.

speculated that a TSE from another species had infected the cows. Because mad cow disease closely resembles scrapie, it was logical to assume that the infected cows had eaten scrapie-infected tissue that somehow mutated into mad cow disease.

Due to biological differences, most diseases cannot jump the species barrier. This means they cannot be transmitted from one species to another. However, TSEs are different. They can cross the species barrier. Therefore the theory that scrapie had affected cows was not improbable. Gajdusek demonstrated that chimpanzees could be infected with a human disease. A few years later he proved it again when he infected another chimpanzee with CJD. In fact, Gajdusek won the Nobel Prize in 1976 for his discoveries.

Scrapie, too, is able to cross the species barrier. In 1950 American scientist Bill Gordon transmitted scrapie to goats by injecting scrapie-infected tissue into the animals' brains. In 1960 Dick Chandler, another American scientist, transmitted scrapie to mice in the same manner. Interestingly, both scientists observed that the disease changed as it crossed the species barrier. For instance, when Chandler first injected scrapie-tainted brain tissue into a group of laboratory mice, not every mouse became ill. However, once contaminated brain tissue from the mice that did

Meat-based animal feed like this may contain TSE-tainted tissue. The disease can then be transmitted to animals that eat the feed.

fall ill was injected into a second group of mice, all became sick. The symptoms the affected mice exhibited and the course of the disease were not the same as in sheep. As the disease changed, its course grew shorter and more virulent. In the mice, the course of the disease took about four months from the time of infection to the animals' deaths, rather than more than a year in sheep.

Cows Eating Cows

Although scrapie can cross the species barrier, it seemed unlikely that infected cows had consumed scrapie-infected tissue, as cows are herbivores. However, since the late 1940s most cows world-wide have been fed a dietary supplement that contains animal protein, which increases their growth and milk production. The protein, known as meat-and-bone meal, is made up of ground-up bones, blood, and body parts of sheep, cows, pigs, chickens, cats, dogs, and roadkill.

The feed is made in a process called rendering, which takes place after an animal is slaughtered. First the animal's carcass is butchered and the meat is removed. Then the parts of the animal that people generally do not eat are put in giant vats, where they are boiled in water. This includes the animal's blood, bones, feet, bladder, tail, and head. The process results in a sludge. The sludge is dried out, ground up, and converted to meat-and-bone meal.

In addition to animal parts that humans do not eat, the car-casses of sheep and cows too sick to walk or stand on their own are also rendered. Known as downer animals, these animals were often used in meat-and-bone meal until recently.

Scientists theorize that because scrapie can cause sheep to be unable to stand or walk on their own, some rendered downer sheep may have been infected with scrapie. Similarly, slaughtered sheep infected with scrapie, but not yet showing symptoms, may also have been rendered throughout Great Britain and turned into meat-and-bone meal. Cows were then fed the infected meal. The infectious scrapie agent mutated in the cows, changing to mad cow disease. Infected brain tissue from these cows, which either were slaughtered before exhibiting symptoms or were downer cows, was then rendered and turned into meat-and-bone meal, which still more cows ate. Indeed, most of the carcasses of the first cows to come down with BSE were rendered. As in kuru, the infection grew stronger and more concentrated as it was passed on.

Changes in Rendering

What scientists still do not understand is why mad cow disease did not appear until the 1980s, as cows had been fed meat-and-bone meal for more than thirty years. Some scientists theorize that changes in the rendering process during the 1970s allowed the infectious agent that causes scrapie to remain strong. These changes made the process cheaper and more efficient. They included the lowering of the temperature used during the rendering process and the elimination of powerful chemical solutions known as solvents, which had been added to the rendering vat but did not harm the cows that ate meat-and-bone meal. Scientists theorize that the combination of high heat and solvents weakened the infectious agent that causes scrapie to the point where it could no longer cross the species barrier. This kept it from infecting cattle that ate meat-and-bone meal made before the 1970s.

Whether changes in the rendering process allowed the new disease to develop was not the only question scientists faced. Because cows throughout Great Britain were eating the infected meal, this would explain why BSE was found in herds all over Great Britain, rather than in one isolated area. It also meant that the disease could quickly turn into an epidemic. In fact, a panel of experts led by Gabriel Horn, a professor of zoology at the University of Cambridge investigating the origins of BSE, estimated that each infected cow that was rendered and turned into meat-and-bone meal infected an average of ten other cows. Making matters worse, scientists did not know how to determine whether an asymptomatic cow was incubating the disease. They did not know what type of infectious agent was causing the disease or how to treat it.

Keeping sick cows from being rendered, scientists hypothesized, would stop healthy cows from becoming infected. But scientists were unsure whether stopping the rendering of downer cows would be enough to protect the cattle industry and the British public. In fact, the Southwood Panel, a group of experts commissioned by the British government to analyze the possible health risks of BSE, had doubts. Although the panel agreed that keeping infected cows from being rendered should protect the public, panel members were still concerned. Sir Richard Southwood, an Oxford University zoologist and the panel's chairman, recalls: "There were enormous uncertainties. And if these uncertainties turned out to be more likely than we had judged there would be catastrophic and very profound consequences."[10] With such a mysterious disease, only time would yield the answers.

Chapter 2

From Cows to Humans

DESPITE EFFORTS TO stop the rendering of sick cows, mad cow disease quickly reached epidemic proportions in Great Britain. By 1993 approximately one thousand cows a week had died of the disease. The rapid spread of the disease as well as its virulence made some experts fear the disease might be transmitted to humans. However, most experts did not think that mad cow disease posed this type of threat.

Growing Concerns

Experts who believed that mad cow disease could be transmitted to humans based their reasoning on the fact that the disease developed when the infectious agent that caused scrapie jumped the species barrier. They theorized that this might once again occur and the disease would move from cows to humans. In fact, in 1988, British experiments proved that BSE could jump the species barrier when the brains of test animals were injected with BSE-infected tissue. Goats, sheep, pigs, mice, and mink were all infected in this manner.

Some scientists theorized that if the disease could be transmitted by injection to so many different species, it might be powerful enough to spread to humans through the consumption of infected meat. The resulting disease, they hypothesized, would be similar to the only human TSE found in the Western Hemisphere, CJD. Richard Lacey, a food science expert and professor of microbiology at Leeds University in England, was quite outspoken about the threat mad cow disease posed to humans. In

1989 he warned: "Virtually all mammals tested were vulnerable, so man is likely to be vulnerable. . . . All evidence so far suggests that humans are not immune from infection. If BSE can be transmitted to humans, the resulting illness is expected to be like our own form of kuru—Creutzfeldt-Jakob Disease."[11]

Lacey did not think the British government was taking adequate precautions to prevent the disease from spreading to humans. Because BSE-infected cows do not exhibit symptoms for years, Lacey feared that infected cows were inadvertently being used in beef products for humans. The only way to stop infected cows from being used in these products, Lacey said, was to destroy all the cattle in Great Britain.

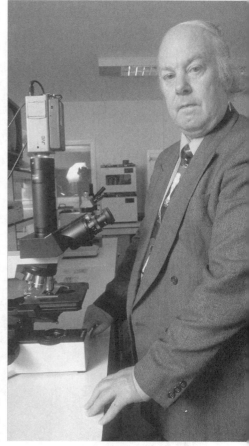

British microbiologist Richard Lacey spoke out about the threat of BSE to humans.

Lacey was not alone in his concerns. The Tyrell Committee, which was formed by the British Ministry of Agriculture to study the impact of mad cow disease, had similar concerns. In a 1989 report, the committee recommended more research be conducted on mad cow disease and better controls be put in place to protect humans. The committee further suggested that all the brains of cows sent to slaughter be checked for BSE whether or not the cow had symptoms. This, the committee said, would show just how many cows actually were infected and would keep infected cows out of the food chain. The committee also recommended the age and symptoms of all CJD victims be monitored for a twenty-year period in order to look for changes in the disease that could be linked to mad cow disease.

The Prevailing Opinion

Despite these warnings, most experts did not think mad cow disease posed a risk to humans. There were a number of reasons for this. First, scrapie had been around for centuries but had never been transmitted to humans even when humans ate scrapie-infected mutton and lamb. Consequently most experts believed that BSE's impact on humans would mimic that of scrapie and thus prove to be negligible. In a January 1989 interview on BBC television, Keith Meldrum, the chief veterinary

In May 1990 a Siamese cat like this one died of TSE after eating cat food made from diseased cattle.

officer of the British Ministry of Agriculture Fisheries and Food, explained: "The evidence on BSE is derived mainly from scrapie, and there is no evidence, scientific or otherwise, that scrapie does transmit from sheep or goats to man. Using this model we are fairly confident that BSE does not transmit to man."[12]

Second, although BSE had jumped the species barrier in laboratory animals, transmission via injection of infected tissue was much more direct and potent than transmission through infected food. A 1988 Ministry of Agriculture Fisheries and Food press release explained: "These results demonstrate that the disease can be transmitted using unnatural methods of infection, which can only be done experimentally in laboratory conditions and which would never happen in the field."[13]

Finally, experts pointed out that it was easier for BSE to cross the species barrier when like species were involved, such as cows and sheep, than it was for the disease to jump from cows to a completely dissimilar species like humans. In fact, in 1991 a British Medical Research Council study appeared to prove this hypothesis. Two monkeys were injected with scrapie-infected tissue, and two were injected with BSE-infected tissue. At the time of the announcement, the monkeys injected with scrapie had died. The monkeys injected with BSE, however, appeared healthy. Therefore, based on monkeys' biological similarity to humans, the experts concluded that BSE could not cross the species barrier to humans. This was proved wrong six months later when the monkeys did die of a BSE-like disease after a longer-than-expected incubation period.

Adding to the controversy, in May 1990 a Siamese cat died of what appeared to be mad cow disease after eating cat food made from rendered downer cows. In the next four years, sixty-two other cats died. All the cats' symptoms were similar to those of the cows. And like the cows, the cats showed no signs of inflammation when examined. Because of these similarities, the cats' brains were studied. The autopsies revealed spongy holes in the cats' brains characteristic of BSE. If the cats had indeed contracted BSE, these would be the first cases in which mad cow disease was transmitted to another species via contaminated meat. Therefore, despite the assurances of experts, the British public became uneasy when news of these deaths were reported in the press.

The British government, however, felt strongly that humans were in no danger of contracting mad cow disease. In an effort to assure the public that eating beef was safe, John Gummer, the Minister of Agriculture Fisheries and Food, appeared on television with his four-year-old daughter, Cordelia. Gummer announced, "My wife eats beef, my children eat beef, and I eat beef." He then took a big bite out of the hamburger, telling the public, "It's delicious."[14]

The First Death

Delicious or not, eating infected beef had risks, as the British public soon found out. In the fall of 1994, eighteen-year-old student pilot Stephen Churchill began acting strangely. "He became quiet, withdrawn and depressed," says his father. "It was a noticeable change. He just stayed in his room, watching TV and sleeping."[15]

Based on these symptoms, Stephen was diagnosed with depression and administered antidepressant medication, which had no effect on him. In fact, in the next few months Stephen began losing weight and complaining of dizzy spells. He appeared confused most of the time, and his memory became undependable. His father recalls: "My wife stayed off work. She took Steve to a supermarket and after shopping they had a cup of tea and a doughnut in the cafeteria. When they left the supermarket, my wife asked Steve if he had enjoyed it. Steve could not remember what they had eaten only fifteen minutes before. This was the first indication of Steve's short-term memory loss."[16]

Making matter worse, Stephen began having hallucinations. According to his family, watching television frightened him. His father explains:

> When watching *Black Beauty*, a children's drama, a little girl was avoiding someone by hiding in a hay loft. Steve became agitated and fearful as though he was the one hiding and under threat. This was a young man who in the past would watch

horror movies with equanimity. On another occasion, Steve was watching *Baywatch* and he felt as though he was drowning when an arty underwater sequence was being shown; again, this behavior was totally uncharacteristic especially as Steve was a superb swimmer. At other times, Steve hallucinated with absolute conviction. These "daymares" as we called them were frightening to observe.[17]

At this point, Stephen's diagnosis was changed to schizophrenia, a mental illness that causes hallucinations. He was prescribed antipsychotic drugs. Once again, the medication did no good. Instead of improving, Stephen developed physical symptoms. He lost coordination and balance. He staggered when he walked. His mother recalls: "About four months before he died, he started to stagger and it brought back memories of seeing the cows on the news. I mentioned it to my husband, could it be this disease that had to do with mad cows? He said, 'No it can't be, it's too ridiculous.' So I dismissed it."[18]

By January 1995 Stephen was unable to walk or speak clearly. He began trembling and jerking his limbs and could no longer feed himself. His father recalls: "His ability to eat grew less and less; his ability to carry out all normal functions waned. . . . It was hard to believe that less than nine months previously this young man had been flying light aircraft. . . . He was confused, dribbling and completely unaware of his circumstances."[19]

Doctors now thought that Stephen's condition was not psychological but neurological. A battery of tests was administered to determine the cause of his problems. Blood tests and a spinal tap showed no signs of infection. Brain scans, as well as tests for HIV and Huntington's disease, a neurological condition, also revealed nothing. The family's genetic history was examined to see if Stephen was suffering from an inherited condition. The doctors were baffled. Stephen's parents were told that he had a progressive neurological condition. Death, they were warned, was inevitable. Indeed, Stephen lost more and more muscle control. In May 1995, eighteen months after first exhibiting symptoms, he died.

Symptoms of Human BSE

First Signs:

- Anxiety
- Depression
- Withdrawal
- Behavioral changes such as short temper
- Weight loss
- Persistent pain and odd sensations in the face and limbs

Neurological Symptoms:

- Unsteady walking and unusual gait
- Sudden jerky movements
- Progressive loss of mental function (memory loss, speech problems, etc.)
- Temperature fluctuations (complaints of being too hot, too cold)
- Clumsiness
- Poor hand and eye coordination
- Headaches and poor vision
- Bad taste in the mouth
- Anger and frustration when unable to complete basic tasks such as fastening buttons

Source: www.hbsef.org.

More Cases

Stephen's was not the only case. Two years before, in May 1993, fifteen-year-old Vicky Rimmer came down with similar symptoms. At first she was confused, anxious, and depressed. Then her memory started deteriorating. Vicky's grandmother recalls one incident in which Vicky missed her ten o'clock curfew. Hours later, when Vicky had still not arrived home, her grandmother called the police. The police found Vicky wandering around the streets of her hometown in a daze. "You could sit and talk to her . . . and still I don't think she'd know where she is," Beryl, her grandmother explained in an article in *Health* magazine. The article goes on to describe another incident: "While running errands one afternoon, Beryl came back to her car to find Vicky gone. She was standing on the sidewalk farther down the street sobbing. 'She was hysterical, said she didn't know where she was,' says Beryl."[20]

Shortly thereafter, Vicky developed problems with her coordination. Vicky's grandmother explains: "She was falling everywhere, like you see those cattle falling. She kept saying to me, 'What's the matter with me, Mum?'"[21]

By August, Vicky was unable to walk, talk, see, or swallow. At the time, her grandmother described her condition in this manner: "She's blind. She can't move. She can't swallow. It's a living hell, seeing her everyday."[22]

Shortly thereafter, Vicky slipped into a coma in which she remained until her death in 1996. By this time, a total of ten people in Great Britain had succumbed to the unknown disease. Among them was Peter Hall, a twenty-year-old student who, ironically, had stopped eating beef because of the mad cow scare. His mother explains:

> In May 1999, I was listening to . . . a program on BBC Radio 4. What I heard horrified me. Being told of a new disease in cattle called Bovine Spongiform Encephalopathy (BSE). It frightened me so much to hear what was being said that I immediately threw out all the beef products that I had in the house. I told my family that I would not be responsible for them eating something that I knew could and possibly would have horrendous consequences in the future. . . . As time went on, I heard about cats becoming infected with a spongiform encephalopathy thought to be from the pet food they ate . . . I congratulated myself that I had recognized the danger in 1989 and managed to keep my family safe. But the warnings had been too late.[23]

Among the other victims were two dairy farmers who had come in contact with infected herds, and two young women, one who had worked in a butcher shop and one who had worked as a meat cutter in a meat pie factory. All the victims had been young and healthy before becoming ill. Many came in close contact with cattle or beef, and all had eaten hamburgers, sausage, hot dogs, and meat pies in the 1980s. The father of twenty-one-year-old victim Donna McIntyre explains: "Donna was always a meat-eater; she liked her burgers and her [meat] pies, but it never crossed our minds that her illness could have had anything to do with that."[24]

Postmortem

At first the deaths were attributed to CJD. But for a number of reasons experts were not satisfied with this diagnosis. Patients with CJD are typically elderly. Yet these victims were all young. Between 1970 and 1989 there were no cases of CJD in Great Britain in people under the age of thirty. But between 1990 and 1995, five cases in this age group had been reported. Four were teenagers. Historically only four teenagers in the world had ever been diagnosed with CJD, and these cases were spread over decades. Indeed, it was very odd for so many cases to occur in young people at one time and in one country. When the first two teenagers had died of the disease, an article in the *London Mail* pointed out: "Some might argue that two teenagers in Britain getting CJD as opposed to four in the whole of the rest of the world was a disturbing precedent on its own."[25]

The symptoms and course of the new disease also differed slightly from CJD. CJD generally runs about eight months, from the time symptoms appear until death occurs. But the course of the new disease was typically twice as long, if not longer. Moreover, CJD usually begins with physical symptoms. Behavioral symptoms develop later. This order was reversed in the new disease. In addition, trembling, uncontrollable involuntary movements, anxiety, and hallucinations are rarely seen in CJD but were present in the ten British cases.

Most telling was the difference between the brains of victims of CJD and the new disease. Because the cause of all these deaths was unknown, the victims' brains were examined for clues after their deaths. The brains revealed a spongy flowerlike pattern surrounded by protein. Although the brains of CJD victims also have spongy holes, the holes do not form a flowerlike pattern,

Britain's Prince Charles examines locally made sausages after several Britons died from eating beef from cattle infected with mad cow disease.

nor do protein deposits or plaques surround the holes. This had only been seen in two other diseases—kuru and mad cow disease. Pathologist James Ironside of the British National CJD Surveillance Unit in Edinburgh, Scotland, describes the brains:

> Even on initial examination, we were overwhelmed by the differences. As well as the spongy changes in the tissue, there were a large number of plaques. . . . But it wasn't just the plaques. They had a particular shape. They were large, they were rounded, and they were surrounded by a ring or a halo of spongiform change. . . . I realized then that undoubtedly this was something different, something new, something very disturbing.[26]

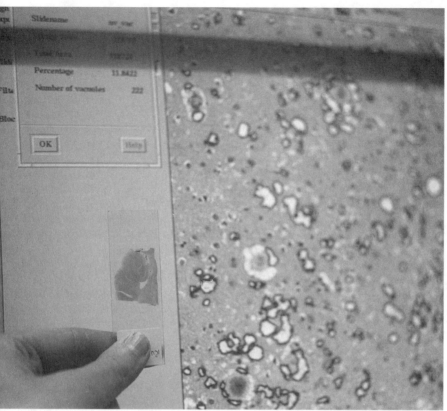

British researchers inspect the patterns of spongy holes in the brains of the human victims of mad cow disease.

A New Disease Is Identified

Because of these differences, it was determined that CJD was not the cause of the ten peoples' deaths. Due to differences in the victims' diet and symptoms, kuru was ruled out as well. The cause was a new human spongiform encephalopathy, which was named variant Creutzfeldt-Jakob disease, or vCJD. Based on the timing of the cases and on the similarity of the victims' brains to the sick cows, scientists at the British National CJD Surveillance Unit theorized that vCJD had been transmitted when the victims ate or came in close contact with infected beef. In a discussion on a PBS presentation, Robert Will, the director of the CJD Surveillance Unit, explains:

The timing of the cases is possibly of some importance, and the reason for that is that if the population of the UK were exposed to the BSE agent in the mid-1980s, it would not be unexpected, if there were a link, that cases would start to occur in the mid-1990s. . . . The striking similarity in both the clinical features and the pathology in these cases suggests that a common agent is operating, and this I think points towards BSE as the likely cause.[27]

As a result of this determination, in March 1996 Harry Dorrell, the secretary of state for health, publicly announced that mad cow disease had spread to humans and the cause was most probably the consumption of infected beef. The announcement

British pathologist James Ironside linked the human deaths to BSE-tainted beef.

caused many British citizens to feel betrayed and angry. They felt the government had put the public at risk by underplaying the risk of eating infected beef. This was done, they asserted, to prevent a health scare and to protect the beef industry.

In an effort to investigate whether these allegations were valid, the BSE Inquiry Committee was formed in 1997. The inquiry lasted almost three years, and the committee interviewed more than three hundred people, including scientists and family members of vCJD victims. The committee concluded that the British government did not act quickly enough in warning the public when evidence that the disease might infect humans started to emerge.

Worldwide Panic

With the discovery that BSE could indeed infect humans, people all over the world questioned the safety of eating beef. Governments passed laws prohibiting British cattle and beef products from being imported to their countries because, at the time, Britain was the only country known to have infected cows. Two thousand schools across Great Britain refused to serve beef in their cafeterias. British fast-food chains stopped serving burgers made from British beef. Instead, the beef was imported from other countries. Some British citizens became more cautious about what they ate, while others gave up eating beef entirely. Mark, a biologist and British citizen, explains: "There was a change in eating habits. All the non-beef sales went up. Chicken became very popular. The processed beef products took a hit. If I bought meat, it would be steak. Giving up beef sausages, that was a difficult one. I do like sausages."[28]

Despite these precautions, between 1989 and 2004 mad cow and vCJD cases appeared throughout the world. As of May 2004, 182,547 British cows that had been slaughtered tested positive for mad cow disease. Infected cows have also been found in Switzerland, France, Germany, Denmark, Belgium, Slovakia, Spain, Portugal, Ireland, Japan, Israel, Oman, the Falkland Islands, and Canada. The largest numbers have been reported in Ireland, where 1,413 infected cattle have been reported. Over

Confirmed Cases of BSE in Cattle

Country	2003	2004	Total since 1987
United Kingdom	611	76	182,547
Austria	0	0	1
Belgium	15	7	124
Czech Republic	4	1	9
Denmark	2	0	13
Finland	0	0	1
France	137	20	912
Germany	54	18	316
Greece	0	0	1
Ireland	182	55	1413
Italy	31	1	120
Liechtenstein	0	0	2
Luxembourg	0	0	2
Netherlands	19	4	75
Portugal	133	17	879
Poland	5	5	14
Slovakia	2	2	15
Slovenia	1	1	4
Spain	167	33	428
Switzerland	21	0	453
BSE outside Europe			
Canada	1	0	2
Falkland Islands	0	0	1
Israel	0	0	1
Japan	4	2	11
Oman	0	0	2
United States	1	0	1

Source: http://home.hetnet.nl/~mad.cow/BSE1.htm.

800 infected cattle were found in Portugal, and France reported over 900 infected cows. However, because only Japan tests all its slaughtered cows, it is possible that other cases went undetected. Moreover, on December 23, 2003, a downer cow in the

A Canadian rancher leads his herd to pasture. Mad cow disease was discovered in some Canadian cattle in 2003, and one of these cows ended up in the United States.

United States tested positive for the disease. The cow was reported to have come from Canada, where another case of BSE had previously been diagnosed.

Human cases have also continued to emerge. Between 1993 and 2004, 140 fatal cases of vCJD have been recorded, according to the Human BSE foundation. The average age of the victims is twenty-eight. All but eleven of the cases have been in Great Britain. Seven of these eleven victims had lived in or visited England during the 1980s and 1990s. The other four victims were French. They had never visited England. Experts suspect these individuals ate BSE-infected French beef, or imported British beef, which makes up about 10 percent of all the beef consumed in France.

As of June 2004, there has been only one death from vCJD in the United States. The case was diagnosed in Miami, Florida, in 2002. Charlene, the patient, was a twenty-two-year old woman whose first symptoms appeared in 2002. She is believed to have contracted the disease in England, where she lived with her family until she was thirteen. In a report in the *Washington Post* her father explains: "She went down very quickly. She lost awareness. She doesn't know where she is and who anyone is. Every day is hard. . . . It's sad enough what happened there [in England]. It shouldn't be happening again."[29] As of the spring of 2004, she was bedridden and unable to speak or control her bodily functions. She was being fed through a feeding tube in her stomach. Doctors said her death was inevitable.

It is clear that mad cow disease has impacted more than just Great Britain. Although at first it seemed unlikely that the disease could infect humans, it can indeed be transmitted, although not easily, to humans who eat infected beef, and the results are deadly.

Chapter 3

A Killer Protein

URRENTLY THERE IS no effective treatment for vCJD and
other TSEs. In order to develop an effective treatment, scientists need to understand what type of infectious agent
causes these diseases and how it attacks the brain. Because
most TSEs can take decades to produce symptoms, for many
years it was commonly believed that a slow-acting virus was
the culprit. However, slow-acting viruses, as well as fungi,
faster-acting viruses, and other infectious agents such as bacteria activate an individual's immune system. As a result,
signs of inflammation and infection appear. Because this is not
the case in TSEs, most experts have come to doubt that these
agents are responsible.

Identifying the Infectious Agent

In 1997 American scientist Stanley Prusiner won the Nobel Prize
for developing a theory that a new kind of infectious agent
causes TSEs. The infectious agent is a type of mutated protein.
When a person eats meat infected with this protein, the protein
begins to change the person's normal proteins, causing TSE.
Prusiner named this mutated protein a proteinaceous infectious
particle, or prion.

Prusiner began his investigation into TSEs in 1972. Over the
next few decades, he closely examined the brain tissue of hamsters and mice that he injected with scrapie. By staining the brain
tissue with a variety of dyes, Prusiner discovered an unusual
protein in the brains of the scrapie-infected hamsters. He named
it PrP protein. At first Prusiner thought this protein was found
only in infected brain cells of hamsters with scrapie. But he later

found that the PrP protein was present in the brains of healthy animals too. The shape of the protein, however, was different from that found in the scrapie-infected brains. Prusiner theorized it was this oddly shaped protein that causes TSEs.

British TSE expert John Collinge discusses Prusiner's theory: "It's a very strange observation that you have these two quite different forms of the same protein with quite different properties. One of them is a killer. If this protein is present in your brain, you're in serious trouble. The other is a normal constituent of all our brains."[30]

American scientist Stanley Prusiner (left) won the 1997 Nobel Prize for Medicine for his discovery of prions, the cause of TSEs.

When Prusiner presented his theory, many scientists disagreed with the idea that a common protein could cause disease. They theorized that the oddly shaped protein was simply the outer covering of a virus. To prove that the infectious agent was composed only of protein and not a part of a virus, Prusiner attempted to destroy the scrapie-infected brain cells with all the known chemicals and processes that destroy viruses but do not harm proteins. As Prusiner expected, the brain cells remained infected. When he transplanted the infected brain tissue into hamsters, they developed a scrapie-like disease. These results demonstrated to the scientific community that prions are composed of protein, that they are infectious, and that they, indeed, cause TSEs. TSE researcher Judd Aiken of the University of Wisconsin in Madison explains: "It's becoming clear that the agent is

An electron micrograph shows prions speckling a cell. The mutated protein specks cause mad cow disease and other TSEs.

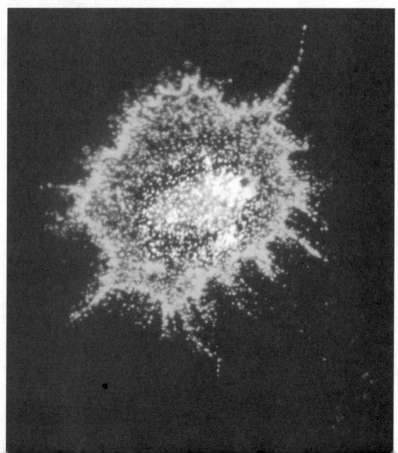

this abnormal protein; it's not formally proven but all data we have supports this idea." He says that most scientists "are proceeding on the assumption that abnormal prions are the sole cause of the disease in TSEs."[31]

The Importance of Proteins

Normal PrP proteins are not the only proteins found in the body. Every cell in the human body is made of proteins. Without protein, cells cannot do their jobs. Among other things, protein is necessary for building bones and muscles, digesting food, clotting blood, and regulating metabolism. In addition, the thought process cannot occur without protein. The brain uses protein to relay signals to nerve cells and for storing memories. Organic chemist and author Robert Hoffman explains: "Proteins are the chemical engine that drives the body. Everything you do from scratching your nose to digesting a pizza is done by proteins. And those actions are enabled by chemical reactions which proteins catalyze [cause to occur]. They produce all the nerve signals. Everything that we are is produced by proteins."[32]

In addition to being made of proteins, all living cells manufacture proteins. In fact, the human body produces more than fifty thousand different types of proteins for different tasks. Each protein is composed of chemicals called amino acids. In order to form a protein, twenty different amino acids link together, creating a chain with smaller side chains hanging from the main chain, similar to a charm bracelet. In forming the main chain and side chains, different amino acids link together in different sequences. This gives the protein different chemical properties. These properties determine the function of the protein. Consequently, a protein's function is influenced by its structure.

No matter its function, once a protein chain is formed, an amino acid on the chain will either pull away from the chain or push into the chain. This causes the chain to fold up into a tangled, spiral-shaped bundle, which looks similar in shape to a twisted corkscrew. Scientists call this shape a helical structure. The exact shape and size of the helix depend on the specific amino acids of which it is constructed.

A laboratory scientist displays a jar containing an infected cow brain. Lab studies on the infected tissue help scientists learn how the mutated proteins function.

Only proteins that have been folded properly can function in the body. Consequently, if a protein has been folded incorrectly and cannot do its job, chemicals known as protease enzymes break down the protein and recycle it.

A Misshapen Protein

Prions are misshapen proteins. They are formed in the same way, with the same amino acid sequence, as normal PrP proteins. In fact, they are identical in every way. However, for reasons that scientists do not understand, when prions fold, they form a shape similar to a flattened sheet of cardboard instead of forming a helical structure. This process is similar to what happens to a child's transformer toy. Although the transformer's parts remain the same, the toy changes into seemingly different objects when the toy is twisted and its shape is altered. Prusiner explains: "Prions do, after all, represent an unprecedented class of infectious agents. . . . Many details remain to be worked out, but one aspect appears quite clear: the main difference between normal PrP and scrapie PrP is conformational [shape]."[33]

Because of their helical structure, which is flexible with many openings, normal proteins can be easily broken down by the body. Because prions are flat, their shape is more rigid and more stable than that of a normal protein. This makes it difficult to break down prions. Consequently, when protease enzymes attempt to break down a prion, its shape makes it impossible to destroy.

Since misfolded proteins are not found in the brains of healthy people or animals, it would seem reasonable to assume that the immune system would recognize prions as a danger to the body and send chemicals to destroy them. However, because prions and normal PrP proteins have the same chemical makeup and

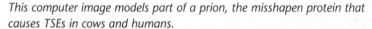

This computer image models part of a prion, the misshapen protein that causes TSEs in cows and humans.

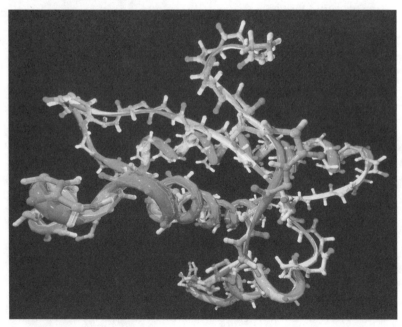

structure, the body does not recognize prions as a foreign substance that should be eliminated. Instead, the immune system treats prions as if they are normal PrP proteins that are produced and needed by the body.

In a 2001 study, immunologist Man-Sun Sy of Case Western Reserve University in Cleveland, Ohio, investigated this phenomenon. In this study, genetically engineered mice that did not produce normal PrP proteins were injected with prions. Unlike animals whose bodies manufacture normal PrP proteins and therefore do not attack prions, the mice produced chemicals called antibodies that attacked the prions. Man-Sun Sy describes the animals' reactions:

> They have never seen a [normal PrP] prion protein in their lives. When you inject them with a prion protein, they think it is a foreign protein. Then they begin to make antibodies like crazy. Normally, if you inject prion protein into you, your immune system will say, "This is a self [normal] protein, I should try to avoid it." But because the mice lack [normal Prp] prion proteins, therefore, they say, "This is something bad." So they make antibodies.[34]

How Prions Spread

Because the immune system does not attack prions, and protease enzymes cannot break them down, they can spread without any resistance from the body. Most infectious agents spread by reproducing. Nucleic acid, the genetic material that comprises DNA and is necessary for reproduction, allows bacteria and viruses to replicate. Prions, however, do not contain any nucleic acid. Therefore, according to the standard rules of biology, prions should not be able to multiply and damage the body.

In fact, before Prusiner's theory became accepted, no one considered that a protein could actually be an infectious agent, because prions do not contain nucleic acid and cannot reproduce like other organisms. In a discussion on PBS, TSE experts Paul Brown and David Bolton examine this issue: "To the best of my knowledge, all infectious agents—all pathogens—require the participation of nucleic acid in order to multiply, to replicate. The idea, therefore, that replication could occur without nucleic acid is heresy. We couldn't figure out, 'How could a protein replicate if it doesn't have a nucleic acid?'"[35]

Yet prions do multiply without nucleic acid. But, unlike other infectious agents that multiply by replicating themselves, prions multiply by transforming healthy PrP proteins into prions. Scientists theorize that prions do this by attaching to a normal PrP protein and pulling away or pushing in, which changes the shape of the normal PrP protein into the shape of a prion. Scientists call this a template effect. Essentially, prions act as a template, or mold, for the refolding of a PrP protein into a prion. Hoffman explains:

> A prion provides a pattern in which the other proteins that collide with it adopt a new shape and become a prion. Suppose you have a plate of cooked spaghetti, which is tangled up and sticky, and you have a plate of uncooked spaghetti, which is lined up side by side in rows. If I took the cooked spaghetti and dropped it on top of the dried spaghetti and started to gently swirl it around, the cooked spaghetti would stick to the uncooked spaghetti. Pretty soon, the cooked spaghetti would take on the shape of the uncooked spaghetti. Some of it would be found in rows just like the uncooked spaghetti. You can think in terms of the uncooked spaghetti being a prion, and the cooked spaghetti being a normal protein.[36]

Once a normal PrP protein is transformed into a prion, it collides with another normal protein and transforms it into a prion, and so on. This transformation is slow when it begins but accelerates as time goes on and more prions are formed. For example, one lone prion transforms one normal protein. The result is 2 prions. Two prions form 2 more prions, and these 4 create 16. Sixteen create 256, and so on.

How Prions Attack

Scientists are unsure how the spread of prions leads to the destruction of the brain. One popular theory is that as prions spread through the brain, they block and destroy nerve cells. When nerve cells are destroyed, they burst or explode. This causes spongy holes to appear where the nerve cells burst. It also causes protein deposits or plaques to form where proteins squirt out. Complicating matters, as nerve cells burst, prions are released into other parts of the brain, where they transform other PrP proteins.

How Prions Destroy the Brain

1 A mutated protein called a prion enters a healthy cell.

2 The prion causes normal proteins in the cell to become prions, too.

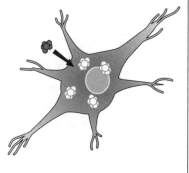

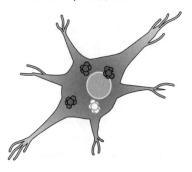

3 The cell is unable to use or break down the prions, and they collect as plaque.

4 The cell dies and the prions are released to infect other nearby cells.

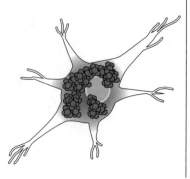

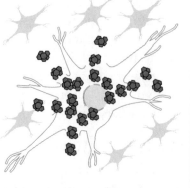

As prions spread, more nerve cells are destroyed. This makes it increasingly difficult for messages from the brain, which are normally transmitted via nerve cells, to reach the rest of the body. Because the transformation of normal proteins to prions occurs one cell at a time and large numbers of nerve cells must be destroyed before the brain's ability to transmit messages is compromised, an individual with a TSE can live symptom free for decades. However, unbeknownst to the individual or his or her physician, prions are transforming PrP proteins and gradually destroying the brain's ability to communicate with the body. Lacey discusses the insidious nature of prions: "If an evil force could devise an agent capable of damaging the human race, he would make it indestructible, distribute it as widely as possible in animal feed so it could pass to man, and program it to cause disease slowly so that everyone would have been exposed to it before there was any awareness of its presence."[37]

Eventually, as prions accumulate in different parts of the brain, symptoms appear. Based on the order in which symptoms appear, scientists can trace the path of destruction, determining which parts of the brain are infected first and in what direction the disease spreads. For example, because memory loss and psychological problems are the first symptoms to appear in vCJD, scientists deduce that the cerebral cortex, which controls thought and memory, is infected with prions first. The prions then spread to the cerebellum. When enough nerve cells in the cerebellum are destroyed, patients start having problems with coordination and body movement. Finally, the brain stem, which controls involuntary movements such as swallowing, is attacked.

A Seemingly Indestructible Killer

No matter in what order prions attack the brain, the end result is death. Prions seem to be indestructible. In attempting to treat kuru patients, Gajdusek determined that most known modern medicines have no effect on prions. Procedures that normally destroy infectious agents have also been proven to be powerless against prions. These include burial, exposure to extreme heat and cold, radiation, and immersion in toxic chemicals.

In his studies of kuru, Gajdusek performed a number of tests on scrapie-infected brain samples in the hopes of discovering a means to cure kuru. In 1988 he tried to determine whether burial, which ordinarily destroys other infectious agents, could destroy scrapie-infected tissue. He did this by covering a scrapie-infected hamster's brain with soil, putting it into a pot, and burying it in his backyard. He left the brain buried for three years. When he dug up the pot, the tissue had deteriorated. He tested the soil in the pot and found it was infected with scrapie.

A shepherd on horseback watches over his flock. Prions that cause illness in sheep can remain in the soil for years.

Originally the infected hamster's brain's level of infectivity was five logarithmic, or log, units. Five log units is the equivalent of ten to the fifth power, or one hundred thousand, which in terms of infectiveness translates to enough infected tissue to kill one hundred thousand hamsters. After burial the infection level was found to be between two and three log units—enough, according to Gajdusek, to kill one thousand hamsters. Therefore, it can be concluded that burial has only a limited effect on prions.

The fact that prions cannot be killed by burial was further shown in Iceland, where a scrapie epidemic developed in 1933 after infected sheep from Germany were imported to Iceland. In an effort to end the epidemic and keep Iceland free of scrapie in the

future, the government ordered all the sheep in the nation slaughtered and their carcasses buried. Three years later when a new flock of healthy sheep was introduced into the country, they too came down with scrapie. Based on Gajdusek's experiment, scientists hypothesized that the new flock of sheep became ill because scrapie prions had survived in the soil where the infected sheep were buried. The prions infected the new sheep when the animals grazed on grasses growing in the soil.

Heat and Chemicals No Match for Prions

In another experiment, Gajdusek put scrapie-infected tissue into a 680°F (360°C) oven for an hour. This amount of heat can melt lead. However, the remains of the scrapie-infected tissue were still infectious, and prions were still active. Gajdusek explains: "Our finding that some infectivity in both crude brain tissue and fibril extracts [infected protein cells] survived a one hour exposure to dry heat at 360°C raises the disturbing question of whether even incineration can be guaranteed to inactivate the agent."[38]

In experiments conducted throughout the 1990s by Gajdusek's colleague, Bill Gordon of the National Institutes of Health (NIH) in Bethesda, Maryland, a scrapie-infected sheep's brain was placed in boiling water for thirty minutes. Once again, the brain remained infected. Other infectious agents would easily be destroyed by such heat in only a few minutes, but not prions.

Gordon also tried destroying prions in a procedure known as autoclaving. This involves using pressurized superheated steam to destroy infectious agents. Autoclaving is commonly used in hospital operating rooms to sterilize surgical equipment. Bacteria, viruses, and fungi are all destroyed after a minute or two of autoclaving. When autoclaving was used on surgical equipment infected with prions, the level of infectivity decreased but did not disappear. And these results occurred after fifteen minutes of autoclaving. In fact, if metal surgical tools come in contact with prions, some prions cling to the surgical equipment even after repeated sterilization. Brown's colleague, NIH scientist Joe Gibbs, proved in a 1976 experiment just how potent prions are. In this experiment, Gibbs used electrodes that had been inserted into the brain of a patient two years earlier. The patient later died of CJD. The electrodes had been sterilized at least three times. Gibbs inserted the electrodes into the brains of chimpanzees. Before long, the animals developed a TSE.

In addition to having been sterilized, the electrodes used in Gibbs's experiment had been cleaned with a form of alcohol called benzene. This powerful chemical did not appear to have any effect on the prions. Therefore, in another experiment Brown tried immersing a scrapie-infected brain in household bleach and other powerful chemicals, including carbolic acid and chloroform, that are deadly to viruses and bacteria. But these substances have no effect on prions. Even formaldehyde, a toxic

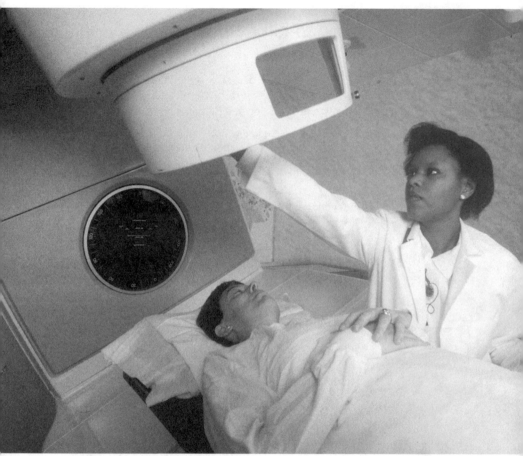

*A patient is readied for a radiation treatment that will kill cancerous cells.
When tried on prions, radiation had no effect.*

preservative that can easily kill bacteria and viruses, has no effect
on prions.

In 1966 two other scientists, Tikvah Alpers and David Haig,
conducted another experiment at Hammersmith Hospital in
London. The scientists blasted scrapie-infected tissue with radiation. Radiation can destroy any substance that has nucleic acid.
That is why it is often used to treat cancer. However, the scientists did not yet know that scrapie-infected tissue lacks nucleic
acid. They were not investigating whether the radiation blasts
would destroy the scrapie-infected tissue. They assumed it

How to Kill A Prion

Effective Methods

- Incineration at 1832 degrees Farenheit

- Exposure to a boiling solution of highly concentrated hydroxide (lye) for at least 15 minutes

- Exposure to concentrated bleach for one hour

- Autoclaving (steam heating) at 273 degrees Farenheit for at least 15 minutes—destroys some prions but not all

Ineffective Methods

- Burial

- Ionizing radiation

- Simple boiling

- Autoclaving for too short a time and too low a temperature

- Formaldehyde or other commonly used disinfectants

Source: http://whyfiles.org.

would. Instead they were trying to determine how much radiation would be needed to deactivate the agent that causes scrapie. However, because prions lack nucleic acid, radiation cannot harm them. As a result, Alpers and Haig found that even high levels of radiation did not lessen the infectivity of the scrapie tissue.

In 1967 Alpers once again tried to destroy scrapie-infected tissue with a different form of radiation, ultraviolet light. In this experiment, Alpers mixed the infected tissue with water and exposed it to a wavelength of ultraviolet light known as germicidal light, which normally causes nucleic acids to split apart. But, as in the first experiment, the infected tissue remained unchanged.

"The Single Most Resistant Organism"

Based on the results of these experiments, it has become clear that prions are almost impossible to destroy. In a 1999 interview Brown describes prions as "probably the single most resistant organism on the face of the earth." He explains:

> You can boil it, you can put it in formaldehyde, you can autoclave it for a little while, you can treat it with the usual disinfectants, you can hit it with ionizing irradiation—and it's like you didn't do anything. You can bury it for two years. This is not to say that some of the agent under these conditions isn't destroyed. But the remarkable thing is that some of it survives.[39]

Although there may still be questions about whether prions are the infectious agents that cause TSEs, the evidence seems to point in that direction. What is clear, however, is that because scientists have not yet been able to find anything to destroy these lethal proteins, prions are unquestionably a very dangerous substance.

Chapter 4

Protecting the Public

SCIENTISTS HAVE NOT yet found a way to destroy prions and thus stop the spread of mad cow disease and vCJD. Therefore, in an effort to protect the public, government agencies throughout the world have passed a number of regulations aimed at keeping mad cow disease at bay. At the same time, some individuals are taking steps to protect themselves.

One of the first steps the British government took was to quarantine and slaughter all visibly infected cattle, as well as those known to be part of an infected herd. This began in 1988. Eventually 3.7 million cows in Great Britain were slaughtered. In most cases their heads were removed and taken to laboratories for study. Then their carcasses were placed into large pits, doused with gasoline, and incinerated.

A Case of Mad Cow in the United States

Other affected countries also took action. In 2003 a cow with mad cow disease was found in Washington State in the United States. The diseased cow was a downer cow that was not identified as being infected until after it was slaughtered. Once the cow was identified, cows in three states—Washington, Oregon, and Idaho—with any link to the infected cow were quarantined. As of spring 2004, out of approximately 100 million cows in the United States, 600 were destroyed and buried in a landfill.

Because scientists do not know whether BSE can be transmitted from mother to calf, 450 calves were among the 600 slaughtered cows. It is believed that one of these calves was the infected cow's offspring, but it is unknown which one. Therefore all the calves were destroyed as a precautionary measure.

In another step to keep the public safe, U.S. agricultural officials recalled more than ten thousand pounds of beef. Along with the infected cow, the beef came from cows that had been slaughtered and processed at Vernes Moses Lake Meats in Moses Lake, Washington, on December 9, 2003, the same day the infected cow was slaughtered. The QFC supermarket chain, which operates eighty-seven stores in the Pacific Northwest where the contaminated meat was distributed, helped in the recall. The chain used information gathered from preferred customer cards to identify and telephone patrons who may have purchased the beef. Brian, a customer who bought some of the recalled beef explains: "That's a call to prevent you from poisoning yourself."[40]

In addition, because the infected cow was imported from Canada as part of a herd of eighty cows, the U.S. Department of Agriculture attempted to track down all the cows in the imported

A rancher watches the burning of carcasses from his infected herd. Measures like this prevent further spread of mad cow disease.

In an effort to stop the spread of BSE, French border guards inspect imported beef to ensure that it is not from a country that has reported cases of mad cow disease.

herd in order to quarantine them and destroy any other infected cows. As of February 2004, when the investigation officially ended, twenty-eight cows had been located and quarantined.

Banning the Importation of Beef and Cattle

Governments around the world have instituted bans on the importation of cattle and beef products from countries with reported cases of mad cow disease. At first this affected just British cattle. For example, in 1989 the U.S. government instituted a ban on the importation of British cattle. Moreover, 499 cows that were imported in the late 1980s before the ban was implemented were traced, quarantined, and destroyed. A year later the European Commonwealth followed suit. In 1996, after it became clear that mad cow disease can be transmitted to humans, the European Union increased the ban to include all British beef products. This ban remained in effect for three and a half years. Also in 1996, 116 cows of British origin were identified in the United States and slaughtered.

Today bans affect other countries. After mad cow disease was discovered in Canada in 2003, the United States banned the importation of Canadian beef and cattle, as did Australia, Japan, South Korea, Taiwan, Mexico, Brazil, China, and others. In like manner, after the discovery of mad cow disease in a single cow in the United States, more than forty countries inaugurated bans against U.S. beef and cattle. As a result, experts estimate that U.S. beef exports will drop from 2.5 billion pounds in 2003 to 220 million pounds in 2004. In addition, in some countries, such as Japan, U.S. meat that was imported days before the ban took effect has been quarantined. The Japanese government reports that approximately 13,000 tons of imported U.S. beef valued at $10 million are stranded in Japanese ports.

More Precautions

Another way governments are protecting the public is by restricting what products can go into supplemental cow feed. As early as 1988 Britain banned the use of downer cows and sheep in meat-and-bone meal feed. A similar ban was instituted in 1996 in the United States. Furthermore, in 1994 Britain banned the use of all sheep, cows, and other mammals that develop other forms of TSEs, such as mink, deer, and elk, in meat-and-bone meal feed. The United States instituted this ban in 1997, and the European Union did likewise in 2000. This step, experts feel, has kept the deadly disease from spreading in the United States. In his announcement of the ban, former Food and Drug Administration

(FDA) commissioner David Kessler explains: "If we don't take preventive action today, we may regret it three or four years down the road. By saying that cattle and sheep cannot be fed any products that cause this disease, we are in essence erecting a firewall that will reduce whatever risk humans have even further."[41]

Even with the ban on the use of mammals in meat-and-bone meal feed in the United States, the case of mad cow disease diagnosed in 2003 made experts investigate what else needed to be done to protect the public. As a result, a number of other safety precautions were put into effect in 2004. FDA commissioner Mark McClellan explains: "Firewalls have been in place for many years. The steps we're taking today are intended to provide even greater security."[42]

The first of these steps banned the feeding of cattle blood to cattle. Before the ban, blood from slaughtered cattle was commonly fed to calves as a supplemental source of protein. Although there is no proof that this practice can transmit BSE, experts say this precautionary measure provides the public with another safeguard.

In addition to the blood ban the FDA also banned the use of ground-up poultry feces in meat-and-bone meal feed for cattle. Chickens and other poultry are commonly fed meat-and-bone meal feed that contains cattle and sheep parts. Then their waste is swept up and added to cattle feed. This is done because poultry feces contain nitrogen, which cattle convert to protein. Experts hypothesize that the manure may contain infected cow tissue that may be fed back to cattle, spreading infection.

Another ruling put restrictions on the way cattle are slaughtered. Some slaughtering techniques, such as using a bolt from an air gun to penetrate a cow's head, cause brain tissue to seep out and enter the cow's bloodstream. When this occurs, the infected tissue can infect parts of the cow not usually believed to pose a risk to consumers, including muscle tissue used in steaks. Now, slaughterhouses must use nonpenetrating bolts. Another restriction prohibits a process known as advanced meat recovery, in which special equipment mechanically removes meat close to a cow's spinal cord. This meat is commonly used in ground meat and sausages and is more likely to harbor prions than meat that is not cut very close to the spine.

The final step taken by the U.S. Department of Agriculture occurred despite the protest of many members of Congress and the beef industry. This step prohibited the use of downer cows in the human food supply. The cattle industry has opposed this ban for many years. Keeping downer cows out of the food supply is costly to ranchers who feed and raise the animals for profit and to slaughterhouses that have to dispose of the carcasses. Experts in the beef industry say that most downer cows are not infected with mad cow disease but rather have suffered injuries such as broken bones. This causes the cows to be unable to walk but does not affect the safety or quality of the beef. Therefore the cattle industry says that downer cows are safe for human consumption. In discussing the safety of U.S. beef, Don Smith, a Texas farmer and rancher, explains: "The big thing that everybody needs to understand is that this country has a safe food supply and the FDA and the cattle organizations and the farm bureau, all these organizations have worked for years to put things in place so that we don't have to worry."[43]

The combination of the work of cattle organizations and the 2004 regulations make most Americans feel confident

Many nations have banned cattle feed made from animals susceptible to TSEs.

Authorities take a sample of animal feed to screen for BSE. Many people believe American beef is safe to eat because of all the testing now done on it.

that they are not likely to contract vCJD by eating American beef. One consumer explains: "Since our government passed these laws, I feel safer eating beef. In fact, I had a steak in a restaurant recently that was quite succulent. I don't feel there's a danger of contracting mad cow disease. All the protections are in place. I'm more concerned with cholesterol in beef giving me a heart attack, than diseases like mad cow being passed on to people."[44]

Testing and Identifying Cows

Some countries have gone even further in an effort to keep infected cows from entering the human food supply. In Japan, for example, the brain of every slaughtered cow is examined for BSE before the meat is deemed fit for human consumption. In the United States, cattle brains are inspected on a random basis. For example, out of the approximately 35 million cows slaughtered in 2003, the brains of about 20,000 cows were examined. However, following the single case of mad cow disease in the United States, Department of agriculture secretary Ann Veneman doubled that number to approximately 40,000 such tests in 2004. Moreover, some meat-packing companies are voluntarily testing every animal that comes into their plants. One such company is Creekstone Farms in Arkansas City, Kansas. John Stewart, chief operating officer of the company, explains: "We believe it is the right thing to do: to test every animal to give the American public and consumers a comfort level that every animal coming from our facility, all the meat coming from our facility, has been BSE-tested and is BSE-safe."[45]

Another significant step that the U.S. Department of Agriculture is taking is the implementation of a national animal identification system by mid-2005. Such a system will make it possible to better track cattle in the United States. Had an identification system been in place in 2003, experts say, it would have been much easier to locate herd members of the cow identified with mad cow disease in Washington State.

An animal identification system involves the creation of a centralized database that electronically tracks cattle from birth to slaughter to food stores. It allows officials to determine within a matter of hours where a cow came from and where it went. In order to do this, radio frequency identification tags are placed on a cow's ear. A calf is tagged at birth and given a serial number. Other data such as the cow's place of birth, age, weight, and medical history are also recorded on the tag. The tags are scanned with a computerized scanning device similar to that used in a supermarket or library, and the information contained on the tag is sent electronically to a national computer database. When the animal is moved to a different location or to a slaughterhouse, the tags are once again scanned, and that information is recorded on the database.

Such a system is used in Australia and Japan. It has not been popular in the United States due to the cost, which runs anywhere from four dollars to twenty-five dollars per cow depending on the size of the herd. Putting the system in place by mid-2005 will cost hundreds of millions of dollars and then about $100 million a year to operate. Easing the burden is the fact that some restaurant chains are encouraging ranchers to use the system by paying a higher price for beef that can be traced from birth. No matter what the cost, the government is adamant that a

Shoichi Nakagawa, Japan's minister of economy, meets with U.S. secretary of agriculture Ann Veneman in 2004 to discuss BSE.

Cattle are now tagged at birth so they can be tracked throughout their lives. Such tracking is expensive for farmers but consumers like the added safety.

cattle identification system be put in place to protect the public. According to a report on the U.S. Animal Identification Plan Information Web site,

> Protecting American animal agriculture by safeguarding animal health is vital to the wellbeing of all U.S. citizens. It promotes human health; provides wholesome, reliable, and secure food resources. . . . Fundamental to controlling any disease threat, foreign or domestic, to the nation's animal resources is to have a system that can identify individual animals or groups, the premises where they are located, and the date of entry to the premises. Further, in order to achieve optimal success in controlling and eradicating an animal health threat, the ability to retrieve that information within 48 hours of confirmation of disease outbreak and to implement intervention strategies is necessary.[46]

Protecting the Blood Supply

The government is also protecting the public by keeping the blood of CJD patients and of people who lived in Great Britain

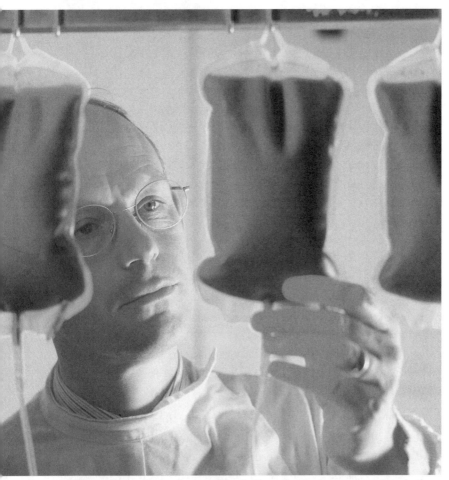

A lab technician checks donated blood. Though scientists are unsure whether TSEs can be transmitted by blood, blood supplies are now inspected for TSEs.

during the mad cow epidemic out of the blood supply. Even before it was confirmed that a British man died of vCJD in 2003 after receiving blood from an infected donor during an operation in 1997, there have been a number of studies and incidents that have caused many experts to question whether TSEs can be transmitted via blood. For example, in 2000 in Great Britain a baby born to a mother with vCJD was also found to have the disease. Experts say that the infection was probably transmitted to the baby through the mother's blood.

Other cases include a 1998–2002 experiment in Great Britain. It involved the transfusion of blood from scrapie-infected sheep to twenty-four healthy sheep from New Zealand. Four of the New Zealand sheep developed scrapie symptoms. Lester Crawford, deputy commissioner of the FDA, explains: "Blood has not been thought to be a source of infection. Now there's new information, which we've been looking at very carefully."[47]

Even before these studies and cases occurred, the American government took preemptive steps to protect the American public and the country's blood supply from TSEs. In 1996 the government recalled all blood plasma donated by people who died of CJD. In 1999 the government took an even more drastic step. It prohibited anyone who had spent six months or more in Great Britain between 1980 and 1996 from donating blood in the United States.

Protecting Supplements and Cosmetics

Because it seems likely that TSEs can be transmitted through blood, another step many countries have taken is banning the use of cow blood as well as cow brains in dietary supplements and cosmetics. In the past these products have often contained these potentially infectious cow parts. Many herbal supplements, for example, contain cow blood and organs, including brains, which may come from any nation in the world. In an article in the *New England Journal of Medicine*, physician Scott Norton found that one widely distributed herbal product included seventeen different cow organs, including brains, spleen, and lymph nodes, all areas where prions are known to accumulate.

Cosmetics often contain cow organs too, and although experts doubt that prions could be transmitted through the skin, some cosmetics are applied to the lips and eyes, where prions might be able to gain entry into the body. As a result, in 2004 the FDA banned the use of cow parts in cosmetics and dietary supplements. The European Union and Great Britain established a similar ban in 1997.

In addition, many countries including the United States have made it difficult to sell cow brains as food products. Some ethnic groups consider cow brains a delicacy. Cecelia, who enjoys deep-fried cow brains, explains: "It's better than snail, better than sushi, better than a lot of different delicacies."[48]

Despite such sentiments, as of 2004 the sale of brains from cattle thirty months or older is prohibited. Cows of this age, experts theorize, have had more time than younger cows to incubate mad cow disease and are thus more infectious.

Better Labels

Changing the way meat is labeled is another way the government hopes to protect the public. Labels on alternative foods are often hard to understand. For instance, although meat labeled "organic" must come from cattle fed on vegetarian feed, almost any meat product can be labeled "natural" as long as it does not contain any artificial ingredients or added color. Such a label does not take into account what the cow has been fed. Experts say there is no consistency in what foods are labeled "natural." Some natural products may come from cows that are never fed animal products, while others may not. In an article on MSNBC.com, Colorado ranchers Roy Moore and Susan Jarret explain: "Virtually any fresh-meat product can be labeled natural. That's the frustrating thing. You can put anything you want on a label."[49]

Therefore, it is not surprising that many consumers consider the current labeling of meat inadequate. New rules clarifying how meat is labeled are expected to go into effect in the spring of 2005. Among the new labels are a "grass-fed" label and a "grain-fed" label. These labels will assure concerned consumers that the beef they are purchasing comes from cattle that have been fed grass or grain rather than animal products.

Some fast-food restaurant chains are also becoming involved in helping consumers to easily find vegetarian-fed beef. The Burgerville chain, which runs thirty-nine restaurants in Oregon and Washington, has started selling hamburgers from grass- and grain-fed cattle. Experts in the food industry predict that other fast-food chains will soon follow suit.

Making Dietary Changes

In addition to buying natural or organic meats, some individuals have taken even more extreme steps to protect themselves against mad cow disease. These people have chosen to stop eating beef products entirely, substituting pork, lamb, poultry, and fish in their place. Others have stopped eating all meats, including meat from mammals and poultry. These people reason that these animals are fed meat-and-bone meal feed and therefore may pose a danger. In fact, according to an article in *USA Today*, a poll taken in England in April 2001 found that 1.5 million people in that country became vegetarians as a result of the mad cow scare. At the same time, experts reported that beef consumption

Cattle fed nonmeat products are becoming popular sources of beef in the wake of mad cow disease outbreaks. Some people have stopped eating beef entirely.

The menu for this Paris restaurant offers no meat dishes. Vegetarian restaurants worldwide report booming business since the advent of mad cow disease.

in Europe dropped 25 percent since the British mad cow epidemic began. A patron of Margutta Vegetariano, a vegetarian restaurant in Rome, Italy, explains that as a result of the British mad cow epidemic, "Business is booming. You need to make a reservation to get in."[50]

It is clear that the threat of mad cow disease and vCJD has led to many sweeping changes. Government organizations throughout the world have taken numerous steps to protect the public. At the same time, individuals have made changes in their diet to avoid infection.

Chapter 5

What the Future Holds

EVEN THOUGH PREVENTIVE measures are in place to protect the public from the threat of mad cow disease, some experts speculate that these steps were not taken soon enough and are not far-reaching enough to prevent a vCJD epidemic. Other experts do not think an epidemic is likely to occur. Because there is no way to predict which of these groups of respected scientists is correct, scientists are researching ways to combat prions in order to avert the possibility of an epidemic. At the same time, they are developing tests to diagnose mad cow disease and vCJD while victims are still alive.

Opposing Views

By looking at possible incubation times of various TSEs, many experts predict that a vCJD epidemic is not likely to occur. They point to the fact that in lab studies in which other TSEs have crossed the species barrier, the incubation time is less than twenty years. Therefore, they say, the worst of the epidemic is over. They also point to the fact that so far every vCJD victim has had a gene that most of the world's population does not have. Lack of this gene, it seems, should protect most people from developing the disease.

Other experts disagree. They theorize that TSEs can incubate in victims for decades before symptoms develop. In kuru, cases with shorter incubation periods were the first to appear. Most of the cases occurred in young people. As the disease mutated, the incubation period lengthened to as long as forty years, and the age of the victims also increased. These experts theorize that the same thing may occur with vCJD. If the incubation period is similar to that of kuru or CJD, then infected people would start exhibiting symptoms around 2015.

Proponents of this theory predict that the majority of the infected people lived in or visited Great Britain between 1980 and 1996 and ate contaminated beef during that time. Most experts doubt that the disease would cause similar problems in the United States, where there has been only one case of BSE. However, people in Europe may be infected. The reason for this is that European countries imported contaminated meat and cattle feed from Great Britain before protective bans were in place. For example, France alone imported about eighty-eight thousand tons of British beef a year during that time.

Experts have no way of predicting how many, if any, people are already infected. The results will depend on how long vCJD's incubation period actually is, the amount of infected meat an individual has to consume to become infected, and the strength of the disease agent. Experts know that cattle can become infected after eating one gram of BSE-infected feed. This is the equivalent of a thimble full. It is unclear if such a small quantity can also infect humans. In fact, all the factors in question are unknown. Therefore opinions on the extent of an epidemic vary widely. Experts have predicted infection levels anywhere from zero to millions. Based on the kuru epidemic, some experts speculate that 1 percent of the British population or five hundred thousand people may come down with vCJD. This is because at the height of the kuru epidemic, 1 percent of the Fore population was infected. Other experts point out that kuru never crossed the species barrier. Such a jump, they theorize, may lessen the virulence of the disease.

In addition a research group from the London School of Hygiene and Tropical Medicine points out that if thousands of people are already infected and the incubation period is forty years or more, most of the infected people will die of other causes before vCJD symptoms ever develop. This makes the possibility of an epidemic unlikely. Only time will tell who is right.

How Humans Contract Prion Diseases

Acquired:

- Diet—eating infectious parts of an infected animal
- Medical procedures using contaminated equipment
- Growth hormone injections

Hereditary:

- About 15 percent of cases are caused by an inherited mutated gene

Spontaneous:

- The prion changes shape for no known reason

Source: http://whyfiles.org.

Preventive Measures Are Not Enough

Another concern is that even with preventive measures, some cattle may come in contact with infected feed. This is because farmers can use meat-and-bone meal feed made from cattle parts in feeding pigs and poultry. This feed may unintentionally become mixed up with cattle feed. Cows may also come in contact with this feed if it is spilled onto the ground. In addition, due to financial constraints, some farmers who purchased thousands of pounds of meat-and-bone meal feed before the ban went into effect may have continued to mix it in with their cattle feed. BSE expert Hugh Fraser of the Medical Research Council Neuropathogenesis Unit in Edinburgh, Scotland, explains: "If you have got to get rid of meat-and-bone meal, you use it. So the stuff continues to flow through the system. And once it started to flow through the system it continued to flow through the system, because there is no policing of it."[51]

Indeed, a report in 2003 by the U.S. General Accounting Office found that FDA inspectors do not test cattle feed. Instead inspectors review paperwork that farmers and feed mills file stating that banned feed has not been used. Although in most cases their reports are true, there is no way to prove it.

Financial constraints have kept the testing of slaughtered cows in the United States to approximately 1.75 percent of all cows slaughtered. Testing cows for BSE before the meat is processed costs about twenty dollars per cow. This cost would either have to be absorbed by the meat industry, which already operates on a tight margin, or it would have to be passed on to the consumer.

This Kansas beef producer tests every animal slaughtered for its beef products as a way of reassuring the public and regaining customers overseas.

The decrease in profits and the increase in beef prices are consequences that many people do not want to pay. A consumer who is also a biologist gives his opinion: "I think the issue is interesting because of the conflict between economics and food safety. How you deal with food safety from animal to consumer is crucial. The monitoring is crucial. The beef industry should provide quality beef. Profit must not be placed before everything else. But, the consumer must be willing to pay his share."[52]

There are many people who feel that no matter what the cost, every cow should be tested before being processed into meat products, which would probably lead to the identification of more cases of BSE. They claim that the current random testing may allow infected cows to pass into the human food supply without notice. Representative Earl Blumenauer of Oregon is one government official who supports additional testing. Blumenauer explains: "Maybe one reason we haven't found many cases of mad cow disease is because the American public is eating the evidence."[53]

The Threat of Silent Carriers

A few experts, including Gajdusek, say that if an epidemic occurs, it will not only affect people who have eaten contaminated beef, but it may be farther reaching. These experts point to studies that show that BSEs cannot only cross species barriers but can move back and forth between species. For instance, in his studies Gajdusek successfully infected mice with scrapie-infected tissue and then used contaminated mice tissue to infect hamsters. Therefore it is possible that BSE can infect cows and then be passed to another species such as chickens or pigs that eat infected feed. Although these animals are not generally kept alive long enough to develop symptoms, both species may become carriers of the disease. This means that even though these animals do not become ill, infected prions can survive in their bodies and be passed on to others who eat them or, in the case of pork, be infected by surgical sutures made from pig intestines. What is even more alarming is that because prions survive after burial, infected chicken feces used as fertilizer may infect the soil

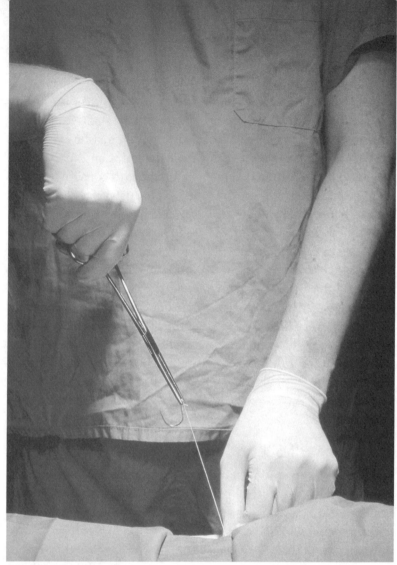

Many possible scenarios for TSE infection exist, including infection from surgical sutures made from pig intestines, a common suture material.

and the produce it fertilizes. If such a scenario is possible, the results could be an epidemic in which even vegetarians could become infected.

Most experts disagree with such a scenario. They cite a number of reasons. First, despite laboratory attempts, chickens have never been infected with TSEs, nor have prions been detected on fruits or vegetables fertilized with chicken feces. Second, there have been no reported cases of a TSE being transmitted through the consumption of chicken or pork. The use of surgical sutures, too, have never been implicated in the transmission of TSEs. Third, with strict safety measures in place worldwide, it is unlikely that individuals who were not contaminated previously will become contaminated in the future. In fact a 2001 Harvard University study examined the risk of an epidemic occurring in the United States. Researchers built a computer model that analyzed the consequences of more than one thousand theoretical situations in which BSE might cause contamination. The study concluded that there was little to no chance of a vCJD epidemic occurring. Researcher George Gray explains: "With the government programs already in place, even accounting for imperfect compliance, the disease in the cattle herd would quickly die out. The potential for people being exposed to the infected cattle part that could transmit the disease is very low."[54]

Dental and Surgical Tools

In spite of the optimism of the Harvard study, some experts are concerned that vCJD can be transmitted via medical and dental instruments because prions can survive on these tools even after autoclaving. Indeed, a 2000 study at Glasgow Dental Hospital in Scotland inspected sterilized endodontic files for prions. These files are sharp dental tools that often prick the gums of patients during root canal surgery. Of the files inspected, five out of twenty-nine used by dental hospitals revealed contamination, as did twenty-two out of twenty-nine used in general dental practices.

Another study looked at the possibility of TSEs being transmitted through open cuts in the gums. In this 1982 study scientists at the New York State Institute for Basic Research for Developmental Disabilities in Staten Island transmitted scrapie to mice by scratching the animals' gums with a scissors contaminated with scrapie-infected tissue. Similar tests in 1999 in Italy yielded similar results.

Despite these tests, there have been no proven cases of transmission of vCJD through dental tools. But there have been suspected cases in which CJD has been passed through surgical tools and electrodes. These cases occurred in Switzerland. In

Dental tools are sterilized in an autoclave. TSE-causing prions can survive autoclaving, but no transmissions from dental tools have been reported.

1974, electrodes were implanted into a CJD patient's brain in order to monitor her brain waves. The electrodes were sterilized and cleaned with alcohol and formaldehyde. Later that year, the electrodes were used on two other patients with epilepsy, a brain disease that causes seizures. In 1976 both patients developed CJD and died of the disease.

What makes these cases worrisome is that if experts are right and there are many people incubating vCJD, dental and surgical tools used on these people may transmit the infection on to others. So too could blood that they unwittingly donate.

It is unclear which, if any, of these possible risks could cause an epidemic. However, scientists are taking no chances. Collinge explains: "We have to face the possibility of a disaster with tens of thousands of cases. We just don't know if this will happen, but what is certain is that we cannot afford to wait and see. We have to do something, right now. We have to find the answers, not only to the questions of the nature of the disease, but to find a way to develop an effective treatment."[55]

Research to the Rescue

In order to combat an epidemic, researchers are working hard to investigate different aspects of TSEs. They are working on

Cow brain tissue is tested for BSE. Researchers hope to soon find diagnostic tests and cures for TSEs.

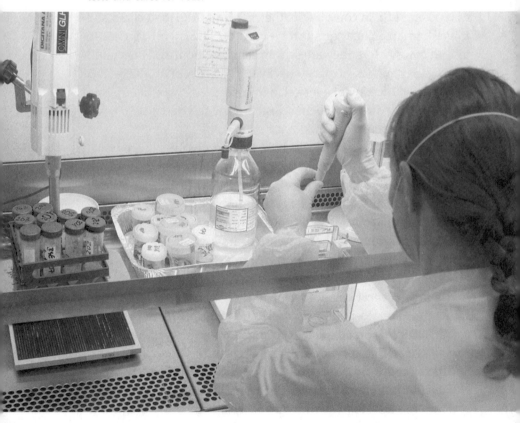

developing treatments to slow or even stop the damage prions inflict on brain cells. They are investigating ways to replace damaged brain cells and developing ways to diagnose TSEs while the patient is alive. Scientists say that if TSEs can be diagnosed early, new treatments could slow the progress of the disease and improve, extend, or even save patients' lives. Moreover, such tests could keep sick cows from entering the food chain.

Because diagnosing TSEs while patients are alive is so important, the U.S. Department of Defense established the National Prion Research Program. The program's goal is to develop a TSE diagnostic test for live patients. In order to achieve this goal, the government has contributed $43 million to the program.

Currently a number of different tests are under development by scientists working in the National Prion Research Program, as well as in laboratories throughout the world. Some are aimed at diagnosing BSE in cows before they can enter the food chain and infect humans. Such tests can be used on farms and ranches to test all cows before they are sent to slaughterhouses. This would be an easier and less expensive way to protect beef products than the proposed testing of every slaughtered cow. It would also prevent healthy cows from being destroyed when one or two cows in a herd are infected.

One test that has already been developed involves the removal of tissue from a cow's tonsils, which is analyzed for the presence of prions. This is done because prions appear to attack not only the brain but also the tonsils and lymph nodes. However, because the test is invasive, it is not always practical. Therefore scientists are working on developing less invasive tests.

Urine Tests

A less invasive test being developed by Ruth Gabizon at Hadassah University Hospital in Jerusalem, Israel, measures prions in urine. In 2001 Gabizon collected urine samples of scrapie-infected hamsters and BSE-infected cows and tested the urine for prions. She did not find any.

Gabizon was not surprised. She reasoned that urine contains urea, a chemical that disrupts the way a protein is folded but

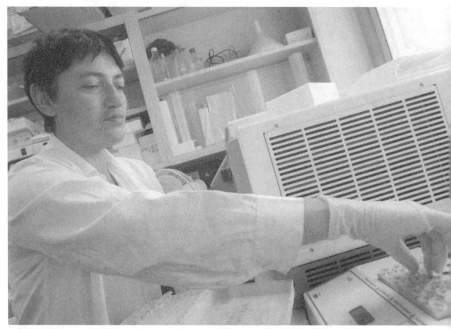

Israeli scientist Ruth Gabizon tests urine for prions. The test she developed detected TSE infection in animals. Doctors hope it will work for humans too.

does not destroy the protein. Therefore the presence of urea makes all proteins in urine, including prions, look alike. Gabizon theorized that if she could remove the urea from the urine samples, any proteins in the sample, including prions, would refold into their original shape, becoming detectable. To test her theory, she devised a method to remove urea from urine samples. As she suspected, when Gabizon retested the urea-free urine, she found prions.

Not only did Gabizon's test work, it was so effective that it revealed prions in the urine of infected hamsters long before symptoms appeared. Moreover, in a blind test in which Gabizon tested urine samples of infected and noninfected cows without her knowing which samples were infected, the infected urine was identified in every case. Gabizon explains: "In the blind test, we quickly picked out the affected animals."[56]

Gabizon is running similar tests on CJD-infected urine. There have been no tests on vCJD urine as yet, and more research is needed to determine if the urine test will work on human TSEs. However, the results of Gabizon's work are so encouraging that Gabizon and her research team are developing a commercial testing kit for animals, which should be on the market soon.

Testing Blood

German scientists at the Robert Koch Institute in Berlin are developing a test that uses patients' blood to diagnose TSEs. These scientists are attempting to identify differences in healthy and infected blood by using a tool called a spectroscope. The spectroscope, which is attached to a computer, emits waves of infrared radiation that molecules in the blood absorb and convert to heat. Different-shaped molecules absorb different quantities of radiation and thus produce different amounts of heat. The heat waves the molecules produce bounce back from the blood sample to the computer and then appear on the computer screen in the form of peaks and valleys, each of which represents a different-shaped molecule. For example, healthy blood containing normal-shaped proteins produces a different pattern of peaks and valleys than blood infected with prions. Therefore, scientists can identify infected blood by looking for specific patterns on the computer screen.

Although this test has not yet been perfected and so far can identify only scrapie, it successfully identified infected samples of blood from scrapie-infected hamsters 97 percent of the time in laboratory studies. Once it is perfected, the test will make it possible to screen donated blood in hospitals and blood banks for any possible TSE contamination. NIH scientist Brown explains: "In a single stroke, it would solve the blood donation problem overnight."[57]

Possible Treatments

Other scientists are trying to develop effective treatments for TSEs. Japanese experiments in 2002 with a medication known as pentosan polysulphate are particularly promising. Pentosan has been used for decades as a treatment for bladder inflammation. Test-tube experiments, followed by experiments on mice, have shown that the medication appears to latch on to prions and stop them from duplicating. The way it does this has not been determined. But when scrapie-infected mice at Nagasaki University were given the medication intravenously via a tube attached to their brains, the animals' lives were extended, with death occurring only after treatment with pentosan was terminated.

The results of the Japanese study are so encouraging that Jonathan Simms, an eighteen-year-old vCJD patient in Belfast, Northern Ireland, is, as of May 2004, being treated with it. So far the treatment, which is considered experimental, has kept Simms alive a year longer than doctors predicted. As in the animal experiments, the drug is being administered directly into Simms's brain. Experts assume that Simms will die if the pentosan treatment is withdrawn. In addition, they doubt that the treatment can reverse the damage that has already been done to Simms's brain, but they theorize that it can slow the progress of the disease. If similar treatment is given to vCJD patients earlier in the disease, it might keep them from deteriorating further. Simms's father notes: "If we can stop this disease now, when Johnny is so far gone, then think what we could have done if we'd only gotten to him sooner."[58]

Indeed, not only has Simms remained alive but, contrary to what experts expected, his condition has shown some improvement. Due to the success of the experimental treatment on Simms, three other vCJD patients in Great Britain are also receiving the experimental treatment as of December 2003. These patients are in earlier stages of the disease than Simms, and all appear to be responding favorably.

Replacing Damaged Brain Cells

As encouraging as treatment with pentosan appears to be, the medication cannot completely reverse brain damage. As a result scientists are investigating ways to replace damaged brain cells with healthy cells. If this can be done in combination with pentosan treatment, patients could conceivably be returned to normal health.

A lab technician prepares slides of human brain tissue. Scientists continue to research human TSEs in order to develop tests, preventive measures, and treatments.

In an effort to replace damaged brain cells, scientists have already successfully injected grafted brain cells taken from organ donors into the brains of patients with Parkinson's disease, another degenerative brain disease. Scientists have not yet treated a patient with vCJD in this manner. Similarly, scientists are experimenting with the use of stem cells as a replacement for damaged brain cells. Stem cells are cells that can transform into any cell in the body and produce new cells. Although the successful application of treatment is still far in the future, many experts are optimistic. Microbiologist and TSE expert Stephen Dealler explains: "In the long term there is a potential for the prions that are being produced in the brain of a person with CJD [and vCJD] to be . . . destroyed using drugs and for the cells that have been killed to be replaced. Only 10 years ago this was thought to be hopeless."[59]

Indeed, the development of new treatments and diagnostic tests gives many people hope. It is true that some experts still remain anxious about the future. However, the creation of new methods of diagnosing TSEs in living animals makes it easier to identify infected animals before they enter the food chain. And, as new treatments are developed, early diagnosis will make it possible for infected people to begin treatment that may extend and improve their lives. In fact, with all the ongoing research on TSEs, there is a good chance that a future epidemic can be avoided and mad cow disease and vCJD will become worries of the past.

Notes

Introduction: A Rare Disease

1. Quoted in Lenore Skenazy, "Beef, Fish, Fowl? It's Not for Dinner," *Albuquerque Journal*, February 25, 2004, p. A13.
2. Quoted in Nancy McVicar, "A Family's Every Day Becomes a Nightmare," Organic Consumers Association, www.organic consumers.org/madcow/nightmare11004.cfm.

Chapter 1: A Mysterious Disease

3. Quoted in Richard Rhodes, *Deadly Feasts*. New York: Simon and Schuster, 1997, p. 172.
4. Quoted in Sheldon Rampton and John Stauber, *Mad Cow U.S.A.* Monroe, ME: Common Courage, 1997, p. 92.
5. Quoted in Rampton and Stauber, *Mad Cow U.S.A.*, p. 92.
6. Philip Yam, *The Pathological Protein*. New York: Copernicus Books, 2003, p. 37.
7. Quoted in Yam, *The Pathological Protein*, p. 14.
8. Quoted in Rhodes, *Deadly Feasts*, p. 34.
9. Quoted in Yam, *The Pathological Protein*, p. 109.
10. Quoted in Yam, *The Pathological Protein*, p. 120.

Chapter 2: From Cows to Humans

11. Richard Lacey, "How Now Mad Cow, Quotations from the Book," Mad-Cow.org, www.mad-cow.org/lacey.html.
12. Quoted in Rhodes, *Deadly Feasts*, p. 183.
13. Quoted in Rhodes, *Deadly Feasts*, p. 184.
14. Quoted in Rampton and Stauber, *Mad Cow U.S.A.*, p. 131.
15. Quoted in Michael Mason, "Mad Cow Mystery," *Health*, July/August 1996, p. 110.
16. David Churchill, "The BSE Inquiry/Statement No 199," Human BSE Foundation, www.hbsef.org/s199.pdf.

17. Churchill, "The BSE Inquiry/Statement No 199."
18. Quoted in Rhodes, *Deadly Feasts*, p. 211.
19. Churchill, "The BSE Inquiry/Statement No 199."
20. Quoted in Mason, "Mad Cow Mystery," p. 110.
21. Quoted in Rhodes, *Deadly Feasts*, p. 188.
22. Quoted in Rhodes, *Deadly Feasts*, p. 210.
23. Frances Isabel Hall, "The BSE Inquiry/Statement No 204," Human BSE Foundation, www.hbsef.org/s204.pdf.
24. Quoted in Stuart Millar, "In the Last Days of Donna, Will Anyone Take the Blame?" Guardian Unlimited, http:observer. guardian.co.uk/uk_news/story/0,6903,375889,00.html.
25. Quoted in Rampton and Stauber, *Mad Cow U.S.A.*, p. 173.
26. Quoted in PBS.org, "The Brain Eater," Nova Transcripts, February 10, 1998. www.pbs.org/wgbh/nova/transcripts/2505 braineater.html.
27. Quoted in PBS.org, "The Brain Eater."
28. Mark, interview with the author, February 13, 2004.
29. Quoted in Rob Stein, "Mad Cow Variant That Hits Humans Is a Puzzle," *Washington Post*, January 3, 2004, p. A01.

Chapter 3: A Killer Protein
30. Quoted in PBS.org, "The Brain Eater."
31. Quoted in Whyfiles.org, "One Heretical Hypothesis," www. whyfiles.org/012mad_cow/3.html.
32. Robert Hoffman, interview with the author, February 18, 2004.
33. Quoted in Rampton and Stauber, *Mad Cow U.S.A.*, p. 122.
34. Quoted in Yam, *The Pathological Protein*, p. 216.
35. Quoted in PBS.org, "The Brain Eater."
36. Hoffman, 2004.
37. Quoted in Rampton and Stauber, *Mad Cow U.S.A.*, p. 15.
38. Quoted in Rampton and Stauber, *Mad Cow U.S.A.*, p. 115.
39. Quoted in Anita Manning, "Prions Survive 15 Years at 600 Degrees?" Mad-Cow.org, www.mad-cow.org/aug99_news.html.

Chapter 4: Protecting the Public
40. Quoted in Peggy Anderson, "Market Chain Warned Buyers of Suspected Beef," *Albuquerque Journal*, January 23, 2004, p. A12.
41. Quoted in Taran Provost, "FDA Acts on Mad Cow Disease,"

Time, January 2, 1997. www.time.com/time/nation/article/0,8599,7427,00.html.

42. Quoted in MSNBC.com, "In Wake of Mad Cow Disease, Limits on Cattle Feed," January 27, 2004. www.msnbc.msn.com/id/4069112.

43. Quoted in Ieva M. Augstums, "Nations Close Their Doors to U.S. Beef," Organic Consumers Association, www.organicconsumers.org/madcow/export122503.cfm.

44. John, interview with the author, February 25, 2004.

45. Quoted in Roxana Hegeman, "Meatpacker Wants to Test All Its Cattle for Mad Cow," *Albuquerque Journal*, February 27, 2004, p. B3.

46. U.S. Animal Identification Plan, "News: Period Extended for Input on US Animal ID Plan, USAIP Executive Summary," www.usaip.info.

47. Quoted in Susan Brink and Nancy Shute, "Is It Safe?" *U.S. News & World Report*, January 12, 2004, p. 19.

48. Quoted in Kimberly Hefling, "Indiana Diners Chow Down on a Disappearing Delicacy," MSNBC.com, January 15, 2004. www.msnbc.msn.com/id/3969530.

49. Quoted in MSNBC.com, "From Organic to Free-Range, Consumers Are Confused," January 19, 2004. www.msnbc.com/id/4001000.

50. Quoted in Ellen Hale, "Europe's Tastes Are Changing," Boje Home Page, http://cbae.nmsu.edu/~dboje.

Chapter 5: What the Future Holds

51. Quoted in Rhodes, *Deadly Feasts*, p. 179.

52. Mark, 2004.

53. Quoted in MSNBC.com, "Officials Investigate Links in Washington, Oregon and Idaho," January 23, 2004. www.msnbc.msn.com/id/4045331.

54. Quoted in *Nation's Health*, "Mad Cow Disease Outbreak Dubbed Unlikely in U.S." February 2002, p. 5.

55. Quoted in Rhodes, *Deadly Feasts*, p. 249.

56. Quoted in Prophezine.com, "Hadassah Team Identifies 'Mad Cow' Protein in Urine," July 2, 2002. www.prophezine.com/

search/database/DailyNews/data/news/994083771.story.
html.

57. Quoted in Adam Rankin, "LANL Scientist Looks for Cow
    Test," *Albuquerque Journal*, January 19, 2004, p. A1.

58. Quoted in Lisa Belkin, "Why Is Jonathan Simms Still Alive?"
    Organic Consumers Association, www.organicconsumers.org/
    madcow/simms51103.cfm.

59. Stephen Dealler, "Potential Treatments That Should Be Con-
    sidered for CJD." Prion Data.org, www.priondata.org/A_
    therapy_explanation_to_patient.html.

Glossary

amino acids: The substance that proteins are made of.

asymptomatic: Without symptoms.

autoclaving: A procedure in which high-pressure steam is used to destroy infectious agents on surgical equipment.

bovine spongiform encephalopathy (BSE): The scientific name for mad cow disease.

chronic wasting disease: A type of transmissible spongiform encephalopathy that affects deer and elk.

Creutzfeldt-Jakob disease (CJD): A rare type of transmissible spongiform encephalopathy that affects one in 1 million people.

downer cow: A sick cow that can no longer walk on its own.

Fore: A native tribe of New Guinea who suffered from kuru.

helical structure: The spiral shape that all normal proteins form.

kuru: A type of transmissible spongiform encephalopathy that affected natives of New Guinea who practiced cannibalism.

meat-and-bone meal feed: A supplemental animal feed made from the carcasses of sick animals, as well as the body parts of animals that are generally not fit for human consumption.

nucleic acid: The genetic material that comprises DNA and is necessary for an organism to be able to reproduce.

postmortem: After death.

prion: A misshapen protein believed to cause all transmissible spongiform encephalopathies.

PrP: The scientific term for protein found in the brain.

rendering: The process in which the carcasses of sick animals, as well as the body parts of animals that are generally not fit for human consumption, are made into meat-and-bone meal feed.

scrapie: A type of transmissible spongiform encephalopathy that affects sheep.

slow-acting virus: A virus characterized by a long incubation period.

solvent: A strong chemical solution used in the rendering process before the 1970s.

species barrier: Biological barrier between different species that makes the transmission of disease from one species to another difficult.

spectroscope: An imaging machine that takes pictures of cells.

template effect: The process in which a prion transforms the shape of a normal protein into that of a prion.

transmissible spongiform encephalopathy (TSE): Any one of a class of fatal diseases that affects animals and humans. These diseases cause holes to form in the brain.

urea: A chemical in urine that disrupts the way a protein is folded but does not destroy the protein.

variant Creutzfeldt-Jakob disease (vCJD): The name given to the human form of mad cow disease.

Organizations to Contact

Creutzfeldt-Jakob Disease Foundation
PO Box 611625, Miami, FL 33261-1625
(305) 891-7579
http://cjdfoundation.org
E-mail: crjakob@aol.com

Provides support for victims and their families, as well as free information.

Food and Drug Administration
5600 Fisher Ln., Rockville, MD 20857
Web site: www.fda.gov
E-mail: webmail@oc.fda.gov

Information about the safety of beef and the blood supply.

Human BSE Foundation
Matfen Court, Chester Le Street County
Durham, Dh2 2TX, England
0191 389 4157
Web site: www.hbsef.org

This organization was set up and is run by the families of vCJD victims. It provides support, personal stories, news, statistics, fact sheets, and an online forum. It also has detailed reports on the human BSE inquiry.

Spongiform Encephalopathy Research Campaign
Anne Maddocks
The Small House
Willow Grove Chislehurst Bromley
Kent BR7 5BS, England

0208 467 3328

E-mail: deal@airtime.co.uk

This organization is dedicated to encouraging research into all TSEs.

U.S. Department of Agriculture (USDA)
Food Safety and Inspection Service (FSIS)
1400 Independence Ave., SW Room 2932-S
Washington, DC 20250-3700
(202) 720-7943
Web site: www.fsis.usda.gov
E-mail: fsiswebmaster@usda.gov

Offers fact sheets and reports on different areas of food safety including beef products.

For Further Reading

Books

Tom Ridgway, *Mad Cow Disease.* New York: Rosen, 2002. A simple book that discusses prions, animal and human TSEs, and the work of Stanley Prusiner.

Lisa Yount, *Epidemics.* San Diego: Lucent Books, 2000. This book talks about different epidemics with a brief section on mad cow disease.

Web Sites

CJD Watch (www.fortunecity.com/healthclub/cpr/349/part1cjd. htm). Tracks CJD and vCJD victims and provides a database. Offers fact sheets, articles, a message board, links, and a victim's memorial board.

Guardian Unlimited (www.guardian.co.uk/bse/archive/0,3332, 210145,00.html). This English newspaper has a large archive of news articles on every aspect of mad cow disease.

Mad-Cow.org (www.mad-cow.org). Offers an archive of more than seven thousand articles on BSE, vCJD, scrapie, other TSEs, and prions.

Many Faces of CJD (www.cpr/798/cjd.htm). Personal stories of CJD and vCJD victims and family members.

Organic Consumers Association (www.organicconsumers.org). This Web site deals with food safety in general. It has a huge database of newspaper and magazine articles on mad cow disease.

Priondata.org (www.priondata.org). Provides news, links, and current research on prions.

Prophezine.com (www.prophezine.com). Offers information on prion research.

U.S. Animal Identification Plan (www.usaip.info). Describes the proposed animal identification system in detail.

Whyfiles.org (www.whyfiles.org/012mad_cow/3.html). Discusses different aspects of mad cow disease, kuru, CJD, and prions. Includes a glossary.

Works Consulted

Books

Sheldon Rampton and John Stauber, *Mad Cow U.S.A.* Monroe, ME: Common Courage, 1997. The authors look at the government's involvement in the British mad cow epidemic and discuss the possibility of a similar epidemic happening in the United States.

Richard Rhodes, *Deadly Feasts.* New York: Simon and Schuster, 1997. This book traces the history of mad cow disease, the scientists involved in its discovery, and the events that occurred as a consequence of the British outbreak.

Philip Yam, *The Pathological Protein.* New York: Copernicus Books, 2003. Describes the effort to uncover and understand prions and new research being done.

Periodicals

Peggy Anderson, "Market Chain Warned Buyers of Suspected Beef," *Albuquerque Journal,* January 23, 2004.

Susan Brink, and Nancy Shute, "Is It Safe?" *U.S. News & World Report,* January 12, 2004.

Roxana Hegeman, "Meatpacker Wants to Test All Its Cattle for Mad Cow," *Albuquerque Journal,* February 27, 2004.

Michael Mason, "Mad Cow Mystery," *Health,* July/August 1996.

Nation's Health, "Mad Cow Disease Outbreak Dubbed Unlikely in U.S." February 2002.

Scott Norton, "Raw Animal Tissues and Dietary Supplements," *New England Journal of Medicine,* 2000.

Adam Rankin, "LANL Scientist Looks for Cow Test," *Albuquerque Journal,* January 19, 2004.

Lenore Skenazy, "Beef, Fish, Fowl? It's Not for Dinner," *Albuquerque Journal*, February 25, 2004.

Rob Stein, "Mad Cow Variant That Hits Humans Is a Puzzle," *Washington Post*, January 3, 2004.

Internet Sources

Ieva M. Augstums, "Nations Close Their Doors to U.S. Beef," Organic Consumers Association, www.organicconsumers.org/madcow/export122503.cfm.

Jim Barnett, "Report Envisioned Annual Loss of $2 Billion in Event of Mad Cow Scare," Organic Consumers Association, www.organicconsumers.org/madcow/billions123103.cfm.

Lisa Belkin, "Why Is Jonathan Simms Still Alive?" Organic Consumers Association, www.organicconsumers.org/madcow/simms51103.cfm.

David Churchill, "The BSE Inquiry/Statement No 199," Human BSE Foundation, www.hbsef.org/s199.pdf.

Stephen Dealler, "Potential Treatments That Should Be Considered for CJD," Prion Data.org, www.priondata.org/A_therapy explanation_to_patient.html.

Ellen Hale, "Europe's Tastes Are Changing," Boje Home Page, http://cbae.nmsu.edu/~dboje.

Frances Isabel Hall, "The BSE Inquiry/Statement No 204," Human BSE Foundation, www.hbsef.org/s204.pdf.

Kimberly Hefling, "Indiana Diners Chow Down on a Disappearing Delicacy," MSNBC.com, January 15, 2004. www.msnbc.msn.com/id/3969530.

Richard Lacey, "How Now Mad Cow, Quotations from the Book," Mad-Cow.org, www.mad-cow.org/lacey.html.

Anita Manning, "Prions Survive 15 Years at 600 Degrees?" Mad-Cow.org, www.mad-cow.org/aug99_news.html.

Nancy McVicar, "A Family's Every Day Becomes a Nightmare," Organic Consumers Association, www.organicconsumers.org/madcow/nightmare11004.cfm.

Stuart Millar, "In the Last Days of Donna, Will Anyone Take the Blame?" Guardian Unlimited, http:observer.guardian.co.uk/uk_news/story/0,6903,375889,00.html.

MSNBC.com, "From Organic to Free-Range, Consumers Are Confused," January 19, 2004. www.msnbc.msn.com/id/4001000.

———, "In Wake of Mad Cow, Limits on Cattle Feeds," January 27, 2004. www.msnbc.msn.com/id/4069112.

———, "Officials Investigate Links in Washington, Oregon and Idaho," January 23, 2004. www.msnbc.msn.com/id/4045331.

PBS.org, "The Brain Eater," Nova Transcripts, February 10, 1998. www.pbs.org/wgbh/nova/transcripts/2505braineater.html.

Prophezine.com, "Hadassah Team Identifies 'Mad Cow' Protein in Urine," July 2, 2002. www.prophezine.com/search/database/DailyNews/data/news/994083771.story.html.

Taran Provost, "FDA Acts on Mad Cow Disease," *Time*, January 2, 1997. www.time.com/time/nation/article/0,8599,7427,00.html.

U.S. Animal Identification Plan, "News: Period Extended for Input on US Animal ID Plan, USAIP Executive Summary," www.usaip.info.

Whyfiles.org, "One Heretical Hypothesis." www.whyfiles.org/012mad_cow/3.html.

Index

Picture Credits

About the Author

Barbara Sheen has been a writer and educator for more than thirty years. She writes in English and Spanish. Her fiction and nonfiction have been published in the United States and Europe. She lives with her family in New Mexico. In her spare time she enjoys swimming, gardening, cooking, and reading.